A New Book of Revelations

of

Revelations

ASHTAR COMMAND

Inner Light Publications

A NEW BOOK OF REVELATIONS

ISBN: 0-938294-85-7

Editorial Direction
& Layout:
Timothy Green Beckley

Cover art by Barbara Lynn

Composition and design:
Cross-Country Consultants
8858 E. Palm Ridge Drive
Scottsdale, AZ 85260

For permission to reprint specific portions or to inquire
about foreign rights, address request to Inner Light,
Box 753, New Brunswick, NJ 08903

Free catalog of books upon request.

Introduction

by Carol A. Rodriguez

This book explains both past (biblical) events as well as events yet to be unleashed during the years to come. While the description of the future that awaits humanity is uplifting and exciting, "Earth's Greater Mission beyond the beyond," the explanation of biblical text in the context of our modern apocalyptic era will probably arouse controversy among readers of a more traditional religious persuasion.

However as most of us read this *New Book of Revelations,* we intuitively find new meaning in the contradictions and lack of consistency found in *The New Testament.* Perhaps we are not so surprised to learn that God's wayward son, Jehovah, inserted distortions into *The New Testament* that have caused all the disunity, divisions and conflicts among the different religions of the world throughout history.

This book represents the apex of Tuella's mission on Earth. According to God (channeled by Tuella), Jehovah tampered with the encodements of Divine Revelation and "as a result the entire Creation has become a battleground for men's minds, a battle of the truth against the false, the Light against the dark, the whole against the broken truth." Tuella was told: "We must change the codes back to their divine state and this is what is represented by your writing." It is now vital that this information be set straight for "the time now approaches so closely to those days described therein, we must now act quickly to release this information for the benefit of My Children, upon whom this clever deceiver shall focus his attention." The present tense is used, as Jehovah is again on the earth plane, physically attempting to thwart the Divine Plan and enslave humanity.

The passages relating to the Divine Plan contain some of the most inspiring and eloquent prose that has ever been channeled: "The American continents are the Great Baskets of My harvest, to magnetize the Light, to contain My Will, and Cradle My Children for Earth's Destiny." What is Earth's special Destiny? We are told that "since the beginning Creation has continued to push outward from the Source in ever greater expansive cycles. Having once again expanded it's self by a great thrust from the point of origination, all of what exists as Creation is preparing to Journey Home." It is at that Moment "when the farthest reaches of Creation quit moving away from the Source, and before reversing direction," that Nova Terra will begin her trip into the unknown.

Who will be qualified to go on this journey to "where no one has gone before?" At that point you, the new agers, the light workers, the spiritually enlightened will decide what you will do. I feel honored to have been able to play a small part in bringing this book before a wider readership. For it is a call to those who are here for the purpose of awakening those who were seeded on this Planet from it's beginning. It is harvest time.

● ● ●

Carol Rodriguez is a New Age artist who has worked on behalf of the Ashtar Command and is a student of psychic phenomena.

Foreword

We welcome once again the opportunity to bring forth a greater awareness of things to come and your role involving Gods plan.

It is time for all those who are on planet earth to start moving forward with their specific role. No longer can you keep saying that all is in order and that all will work itself out. You are the workers who have accepted the responsibility for doing this. We can only support your efforts. You are the ones who take the lead in the third dimension. We have prepared the way from above but it takes the preparation from below to bring the two worlds together. You must remember why you are here.

Let us begin by stating how important it is not to get involved in the events of the world. There is a need to know what is going on but don't get attached in any way to the results of what man has created. The entire focus must now be on God's plan and this is where all focus must begin and end.

You will do well not to involve yourself with the affairs of others who are trying to get their act together so to speak. You can easily try to help those who are not yet truly ready for help and this will only delay the most important work that you have before you. You will also do well not to be too concerned about your personal affairs. They are all being taken care of. We can see profound changes in the inner workings of your beings and are most pleased about your progress. We encourage you to continue on full steam ahead. Times continue to move on at a very fast pace. The planet is going through complete destabilization this year. Such of your prophesy for this past year has been delayed by the forces who are working against the Father's plan. There is a desire by some to see a big BLAST rather than a smooth transition. Perhaps they still want the drama or perhaps they don't want to see the transition at all. But the forces which must be unleashed will be released in the coming years. This process can not and will not be delayed any longer. Your roles all revolve around many of these changes so awareness is important.

You came here to bring about an awakening to those who were seeded on this planet from its beginning. You are now being asked by those of responsible for this planetary mission to bring forth this awakening. You can only do this if you yourselves are fully conscious of how this process works with your own being. This is why you have been kept in the dark, sort of, for so long. Now you are being awakened through the efforts of all those associated with this mission. You will all go through profound changes in the coming days and weeks. Don't try to resist these changes because they are what you have all been waiting for. Now is the time to prepare yourself for that which is to come. Many changes will also be happening around you (versus internally) which will bring about an awareness of the things which must take place. In other words what you see taking place in the external world around you will bring a sense of action to you in which you will begin to see that which you came here to do. This will all be much CLEARER as you allow the process to take place.

It is time for those residing on this planet to know that God exists in all that is of the light and it is time that those on the earth who hear this message know that God is calling them forth into the higher realms. You have all worked together in many different assignments on behalf of God during the many eons of your existence as individual entities. Before you were given birth through this individualization you were in fact part of the energy which is now identified as God. Thus you carry with you in your identities the element of God which is Lord Jesus. In other words as you walk on earth you are representatives of this energy force which has the power to transform that which is not in harmony to a more perfect state.

You are now being called on to recognize your Divinity and to understand the meaning of this current experience you are engaged in, in the physical plane. You are being called on to feel this energy force through your being and to recognize its source. You are light beings and this physical experience is only to enable you to serve the Father/Mother Creator of All. By holding this God energy on the planet you are facilitating the transformation of the planet and those who reside on it. You can begin to recognize what this involves in terms of the greater aspects of your collective mission.

First you must recognize that as you anchor this energy you are in fact facilitating the Divine Plan which you have so faithfully carried out in the past. You have come together now to complete that which you have started when this planet came into its existence. This was the first time when you acted as Creator Gods in this universe and you have truly supported the creation of the most magnificent expression of God in the form of planet earth. You have not been as involved with the spiritual development of specie until your most recent incarnations when you chose to bring forth a higher consciousness to those who were ready to receive it. Now you have returned to help in the harvest of those who have received this higher consciousness and to help in the process of bringing forth a greater awareness of things to come in the future.

You have also come here to help in the physical preparation of the planet for the end times which will support the process which will enable the planet to enter into a higher state of consciousness for the planet is also a living expression of the Creator. It has been the plan all along to bring the planet into a higher vibration of existence whenever circumstances provided for this opportunity. THIS IS THE LAST OPENING FOR SUCH A TRANSITION DURING THIS COSMIC CYCLE. In other words the planet must go through a transition at this time regardless of whether or not the specie is ready to move forward with it. As you see today mankind has not been able to fully accept the lessons of the past and is not ready as a collective consciousness to enter into the higher kingdoms that God has prepared for them. So we are now faced with the decisions which are necessary to accommodate that further development of the specie on other planets which are provided for this purpose.

You will take part in helping those who need such experiences to depart from this planet when the time draws near. You will also help those who are ready to enter into the higher kingdoms to make their final preparations. You have all been through this before and now once again you must become aware of what needs to be done. You have all been captivated by the experiences of the physical plane and you have all enjoyed the experiences of life. This will continue but you will now enter into a new phase of this life expression in which you will bring forth that which is necessary for these times. We suggest that you focus on your purpose and the Father's desire for His children to be in total balance to receive Him. He is most concerned about this balance as you are well aware of. It is most important that all be made ready for the personal ascension of the individual in his departure from this planet. The best way to prepare is to make ready the light body. By staying in tune to our energies you remain clear. Light workers are not all going to understand the importance of completing that which they agreed to do. There is not going to be a middle ground in this area. Either the work gets done by those who agreed to do it or it must be done by others who will come in the event that they have to.

The following weeks will be very trying on your souls. Accept much change and know that all is in order for the final days. We stress that you each stay focused on your mission. You must be able to see the detail which is now necessary for your completion of that which you came here to do. Now is the time to bring the final preparations for the mind body and soul to inherit the spirit body.

It is not only the dark forces that are causing difficulties but, as you know, certain Light Workers have once again begun using ego enhancements along with the power that they have been entrusted with. We are very concerned that those who are misusing power do not continue to do so.

Let go of all the intellectualism that is confronting the awakening process. The books, the seminars and all the interactions have served their purpose up to now. But NOW you must take note of your specific role and then take action.

Channeling is another one of those items which has served its purpose. The only channeling that should be addressed is the individual experience with the Father; He who has Created ALL.

There is no authorized channeling to be continued unless it is with the Fathers personal and direct approval. There will be some who are permitted this activity as you refer to it. What must be acknowledged is that you are all being made ready to speak the words of God directly through your vessel. Channeling is not going to be the method but rather the opening up to the direct energies of the Father (i.e. no middle men).

Now is the time to take note around you and see what it is that needs to be changed. Don't accept things which are less than harmonious in your life. You have all been through a lot. It will not be the time to reflect on the past, for now is the time to move into the future. We have all been waiting a long time for these coming events which are now upon us. You must be ready yourself in all ways. WE WANT YOU TO KNOW THAT WHAT IS ABOUT TO COME WILL BE VERY CHAOTIC TO THE ENVIRONMENT IN WHICH YOU RESIDE and it is very important that you take the time to sit with these messages to see how you feel.

You will begin to sense a NEW BEGINNING for all that you are currently involved in. You will also see where it is that you must be and for what purpose. You will acknowledge that you are truly great beings who have chosen this mission because you above all others could complete it. If it was not necessary that you come here but it was your desire to assure that what was started would be finished. Now is the time to complete that which you came here to do.

We are the Lords Jesus and Michael always at your service We only ask that you allow us to help you.

Introduction

A joint statement from the Lords of Light, through the Throne energies of Lord Michael and Lord Jesus Christ, through messengers Tuella and Obid.

We wish it to be known at this time that the Light Workers must get their acts together so to speak. These games that continue to go on are in direct confrontation with the Father's will for this planet. It can become a great obstacle for all of us if the Light Workers do not get on with their real work or get out of the way; as they are truly missing the opportunity as it opens before them.

These games are those which have been demonstrated through the misuse of the powers which have been brought forth. At this time The Light, which now penetrates the planet, carries with it much knowledge and this knowledge is what is being misinterpreted and projected to others in the physical plane, causing distortions and missed opportunities which were provided for the benefit of the planetary mission.

We address this misuse of God's power in the form of the Light rays as one of those things which should have been learned during many similar situations on the planet. This includes the time of Atlantis and Lemuria when these same powers were provided from the Throne and misused by the fallen ones who have now come again to serve and balance out their karma. These are not the same as those thought forms which have come here to your planet to specifically cause chaos and confusion and to deny the evolutionary process to continue.

Those who consider themselves channels must look beyond that which they are "channeling" to see what the specific purpose of the message is. Those who just bring information or entertain others are not doing any service *unless it is within the full context of the Father's will.*

Each will have their own method and will have to touch base with the Father to know the direction. It is enough to know that the Father is listening to each one of you and that he will carry forth that which is necessary for the individual's departure. You are being asked to *tell this to the masses at this time* for it is very important for them to know this.

This contact of this moment is considered channeling in the sense that you are joining those who communicate with the higher energies of the Father. What makes the difference is that you are fully conscious of the communication and are working in behalf of the Father's plan. (A) You are not using the information to glorify your own egos nor are you. (B) using information which is from a lower energy form which is the source of most of the information that is being passed around at this time. The channeling that we speak of is that which is (C) represented in trance mediumship as well as that which is being purported from the Father. He the Father only speaks with those who will listen. If one chooses only to hear what it is that they desire the Father will not allow them to bring that which you too by example are being entrusted with. There is much to understand here about the Father's way. He will never allow the ego to be the dominant force in the representation of his energies in any realm. It is the ego which distorts and that is why the Father uses only those who are free of the ego to bring forth his messages for the masses.

You are here also to bring about a *certain consciousness* among those Light Workers who are here to help in this transition process. This is important in that there is much work to do in your dimension. This is why the Light Workers came in the first place. Now they must acknowledge the work that they came here to do or make themselves ready for their departure. Either choice is an important one and we will be encouraging you to bring forth this message to those who will listen.

You may also wish to know that there are many who would like to see you "lost in their own truths." Do not be sidetracked by others who are also entangled in their limited thoughts which will prevent them from seeing the truth.

There are those who are supposedly committed to being the

Light but have refused to pick up on the need to fulfill the Father's will. We are not going through an exercise of awakening souls only to have them sit and remain idle in the face of much work. This has been a very trying experience for all those in the higher realms who have given their all to this mammoth project only to find that those who have been receiving the benefits of this effort have failed to realize their role in this project.

You are now ready to lay it down as you see it. And you Tuella and Obid will remain in the presence of the Father to do His will. The time has come for us to pull back our energies and let the chips fall where they must with those who are simply unwilling to directly commune with the Father and with those throne energies that represent the God self in each and every one of us. We will not support the efforts of those who are only going to use the truth to enhance their own egos or who will just remain doing their own will. This is not a project of individual wills but that of One, and this one is the Father/Mother God who has been and will always be the creator of ALL. Only when man gets down from his pedestal will he be able to realize that this is a very serious mission. We have allowed the process of awakening to go forth as it has been because it was seemingly the only way to get the Light Workers aware that God even existed and that we were here to help in God's plan.

The Light workers have distanced themselves from God in the wake of their awakening in order to preserve their "new found" *identities*. This is where the process begins to break down, as it has always done on this project involving planet earth. As soon as the awakening comes then the process of using the new found knowledge begins to proceed forth with *human will* versus God's will. How many times have we seen this on this planet? How many times did we have to keep reminding those of the times gone past? We certainly have given enough examples to the many who have asked. Now we are once again faced with the problems associated with the awakening and the powers that have been drawn forth.

You must remain centered in Light during all this confusion among the Light Workers. We suggest that you continue to point out that we will not support the process of channeling where any individual is using the information for personal gain or without full responsibility to the Father and His will. In the past channeling has been used because it was one of the few forms which was working in the awakening process. We have had many good messengers, but now those genuine messengers are removing themselves from the public eye and those who remain are working with energies less than those of the Throne.

We caution all, that psychics cannot and will not be a source of Divine truth. They can only register thought forms which remain in the energy field of the third dimensional being. They are not capable of reading the Divine blueprint. This is reserved for the soul and only the individual process of communing with the Father can reveal one's purpose. This is for a good reason, because only with this process can one be assured on knowing their Father in heaven. If the external source were capable of handling this knowing process for another, then things would be different but this simply is not the case.

We also caution you in respect to those who desire you to "entertain" them with the Truth which has been revealed to you. We will not allow these truths to be used in this manner. They are for those who are committed to serve and only for those committed to serve. This information is being brought forth at this time only because it is a necessary part of the process of the committed worker. It is part of the Light Body activation process as well as part of the mission itself.

God has ordained that certain teachers come forth at this time to bring clarity to channeling God's message. These teachers have been certified by I and Lord Michael. We have permitted only the worthy to go forth at this time with the word. God has pulled back all the channels that have been used in the past to make ready for these messengers who are of the higher order. This is why we have been explaining this issue of channeling to those who are relying so heavily on it. The channeling must stop and those who can speak the words of God must be ready to do so. You have both been ordained to do so, and are being prepared to do so at this time. Needless to say you have both been "certified" for this mission.

Those who work to become known, to achieve popularity or ego satisfying purposes to open wider doors are lesser thought forms. If there is not the necessary clarity, all is lost. Clarity of purpose must awaken to achieve the Father's desire. We are most concerned about this lack of understanding purpose.

THE FOCUS MUST BE ON GOD. ONLY GOD WILL DIRECT THESE FINAL DAYS AND THAT WHICH MUST TAKE FORM. ALL OTHER ENERGIES MUST TAKE NOTE OF THIS. WE WILL TOLERATE NO INTERFERENCE BY THOSE WHO ARE OF THE LIGHT BUT NOT FULLY AWARE OF THE FATHER'S MISSION.

Section 1

Our Fathers Unveil's The Great Deception

"Love Letters From The Throne"

I AM THE FATHER-MOTHER GOD. I AM *the total Source of All That Is. The Supreme Creator above All. I call to MY Children. I want you to know that I Am HE whom you must come to know in a more personal way. MY Throne energies are with you to support this process.*

I want so much to communicate with all of you as often as you will permit ME. I long for your Love as you may long for Mine. I have created you in the desire that you come to know ME.

Let us share in this life together and Love one Another as well as we have so often done before. Many of you become so busy on behalf of MY work, but it is your Love that I long for. MY Business must make way for our time together, if it is your desire to be near ME.

I see the beauty in all of you and know of your abilities. I will be with you always and whatever your decisions are I will follow them with great support. I will accept them regardless whether they are of MY will. I have given you this power to make your own decisions and if it is your will, so it is MINE. I trust in all that you do and know that we will come together very soon.

You are truly MY Chosen Ones. I have sent you forth from MY Throne to handle these difficult times for this planet. I will never forsake you nor let you down. Go forth knowing that the end is near and the time for rejoicing is at hand. I AM with you and I will share in your walk and overshadow your footsteps. I will always give you what you seek. I will always answer your call.

I share every feeling from your heart and welcome your

16

thoughts to ME as you walk through these final days. Much will take place and for all of US. We will shed the tears of Love as well as the Joys Of Love. I will be with you as you walk through the Universe each night. We shall sit and prepare the Feast. We are as ONE...I LOVE YOU. The pathway is simple and the Lights are turned on more brightly than at any time in earth's history. Welcome this Light into your life.

We have been through much together. I welcome you HOME, knowing that you have all been faithful servants who have always responded to MY CALL.

• • •

Corruption of the Light Codes of Creation
Part I

1. My Child shall we begin. We are setting into position this vortex for you within which we shall work. This requires nothing on your part. My Sons shall do this thing and you will receive My Words more clearly, more powerfully. Our evening talks will not be lengthy. We will slowly build up a context of My planning.

2. First of all let me introduce you to some of the subjects we hope to cover in the coming months. As you know I am most concerned about getting a wedge of truth concerning the Jehovah confusions into the minds of those who are ready to accept the Truth. This subject has many lessor subdivisions and covers a very broad territory.

3. We need to consider first how the errors originated and why. Then we examine the implantation into the third dimension and is progressive expansion. The scope is tremendous. Everywhere there are souls where you will find the errors made a permanent part of all knowingness.

4. This My son Jehovah whom we call by another name has been having a free reign over My Children for many eons and ages. His dark deeds were allowed to grow and flourish in the thinking minds of man on earth as a proving ground for their willingness to search for Me and to find and know My Love for them. For millions of years thousands of ages of cycles of time, they have again and again set themselves to attempt to understand Divine revelation. But the encodements were tampered with and corrupted before the thought forms were ever released to them. As a result the entire Cre-

17

ation has become a battleground for men's minds, a battle of the truth against the false, the Light against the dark, the whole against the broken truth.

5. It is My intention to work with you my Child and carefully construct for your presentation a complete analysis of this entire projection, and to step by step go through the points of emphasis so that thinking souls can follow our work and come to an understanding of the perversion that has taken place.

6. I have sent many of My Sons and Daughters into the negative and antagonistic atmosphere of this planet for the purpose of counteraction against the confusion. But hitherto little has been accomplished yet I have not in any sense lost control of My Creation.

7. I have dared to permit the infiltration of corruption of My Design and My Words to experience that which man has chosen to call the freedom of will or the power of choice. Therefore I have permitted Jehovah free reign in his deeds for an unaccountable length of earth cycles to prove the is end to him that nothing he has accomplished will stand against the Love I have planted within my Creation which will ultimately be fully expressed and understood by all.

8. I have loved him as I have loved all My Sons. I have given him permissive leeway to experiment in his folly to seek to set into motion an Anti God Order in the Universe which would be designed to overthrow My care over My Creation. Now it is that point in Time for this Creation when the experiments must stop, when the accounting must take place and the blessed Planet be released to her Destiny in My Divine Plan. Therefore this bizarre farce that has gripped all of Creation must now be shakened and loosened from the reality of humankind and the crooked things must be made straight, the way must be made plain and My son Jehovah must face his consequences and his Great Lesson. He has not before this time been called unto this reckoning, but now he also must come under the powerful incoming rays of Great Light being shed forth through all worlds to prepare for the New Order in the Universe which shall operate under My Creative Principle of Total Harmony and Balance.

9. Every smallest fragment of Life upon this planet, be it but the blade of grass, carries the Divine Imprint of its cell its unit of Life. Its encodement, its ongoing creation is written within its Life nucleus. But too many times has this encodement been trifled with, distorted and

made to function in a manner that was not MY inten. In cycle following cycle again and again a false structure has been superimposed upon the Life Unit and perversion has been released into My handiwork.

10. Now is the hour in the history of Earth when all of these perversions shall be cleansed away, removed if necessary, and the correct encodement reinstated that will permit all of Life, all cells, all units, to return to the original design and Creation itself reflect an Earth returned to Perfection.

11. Jehovah was able to alter the genetic coding of those on the Earth plane so that they would be unable to return to their greater awareness during the end times. He was aware of the Plan, and altered the course of the Plan through his ability to alter the Light Codes of Creation. Now with the cleansing of the Heavens, these codes cannot be altered anymore. However, the codes have been altered in the pest which have affected all of Creation in the moment. We must change the codes back to their Divine Slate and this is what is represented by your writings.

12. Therefore have I stated, therefore have I promised that All things shall be made New. Behold I create a New Heaven, a New Earth, and My people shall be My people and I shall truly be their God with no usurping of My pure Fatherhood any longer from one who rises to destroy this goal toward Oneness and Harmony throughout this Omniverse.

13. The time has come to extend once again to My son Jehovah, whom I love equally as all others, that opportunity to experience Love, if that be possible, and to extend My Hand unto him to return to the Father's table to partake of the Father's Feast and to enter into the Joy of all My Sons and Daughters who will sing for Joy within the New Creation.

14. He has distorted the truth from which others are basing their understanding of the Fathers Plan. As we attempt to bring forth the truth there will be attacks from all Earth religions for Jehovah is within all teachings. He will try to affect your mission by attempting to remove you so to speak. He listens to the messages of the Universe which this correspondence with you represents. While it is true he is a Being of Power, yet he knows not the Power of Love. He can not conquer Love but he will try, and his trying will cause the confusion and sorrow that follow for those without true discernment. Discern-

ment and guidance can only come from within in these latter days. It is the only source anyone will be able to safely draw upon. The Throne Connection is to help lead the Way to go within.

15. Therefore to present him this opportunity it is necessary that the Truth be made right, that the lies be exposed, that the insidious plot of a million centuries be uncovered to the Light of the New Day, that all mankind as well be given the opportunity of choice, choosing to be with Me in the New Creation. Unto whomsoever will, I will extend the invitation to find their Truth in in Me. This shall be the purpose of Our coming work and yours shall be the human energy that shall be My instrument in bringing this important cleansing to the minds of mankind. Let us therefore gather Our Forces and dedicate Ourselves to this great task, that we might find and enlighten all of those whom I have sent unto the dark highways and byways to return to Me My seed from the Harvest. With these words I close this first session. I AM the Father-Mother God Creator.

I Am A Loving Father
Part 2

1. I AM the Father Mother God who speaks. We continue Our discourse concerning those things which must be written to My Children. I have proposed in Our last conversation that we must first consider what has taken place within the minds of men and why it has been brought by My son of My Own Being.

2. I speak of that one whom the world calls Jehovah. In the beginning of the times of Joshua and the need to settle the multitude into a semblance of order, and the beginning of nation, Joshua was My representative, My spokesman to the people appointed by Moses in the authority vested in him by Me. His brother Aaron was appointed to serve the Priesthood and attend the altar, thus the work began.

3. It was at this point when, after Moses was removed from the leadership, that the voice of Jehovah entered the scene and usurped My Voice to inject his perversions of principles and precepts. My Love for those whom I had led so gently into their New Land was overpowered by the severity of the Jehovah entity's wrath upon the people and harshness in handling their guidance. The Ark became a tool of destruction because it was used in ways for which it was not created. The Ark became used by those who sought to control the planet and not by My Forces of Light. This is the reason it was removed from the hands of those who sought to limit the creative process of the planet. It was removed by the Space Brotherhoods of Light at My request, along with the many other tools just like it. At the time I originally placed it in the tabernacle *it was already in the consciousness of man that they could talk with the Father! The Ark was used by the fallen thought forms who were shut off from the communication with the Father through their own desire to not recognize their Father!* The Ark was then used to communicate with beings that were less than Divine, who were only in contact with Earth through this tool and others like it. Within the present psychic community this same situation prevails with all of their gadgets and gimmicks for the purpose of avoiding a true going within and direct confrontation with Me, their Father and Indwelling God.

4. This intrusion of direct manipulation of the nation projected into the religious world of the time with a far reaching influence upon all other nations and peoples that surrounded My Flock. As many generations came and departed I resolved that an Intercessory Action was required. I had manifested the twelve tribes to bring about a genetic upgrading to the consciousness of souls upon the planet to offset the forces that were then genetically being cloned and brought forth by he whom you call Jehovah. My Intercessory Action was manifested as the Voice of My Great Judges and Prophets whom I gave to the people throughout the centuries to bring them the pure words of My Love and the paths in which they should walk. These were also sent to point their thoughts, their hearts toward Another that would come: as in the sweetness and gentleness of Isaiah's words and the Psalms of My beloved son David.

5. The wider world soon became attached to these recordings of holy words with much Love for them and the hope they brought into the human scene. But the conception of Me as a Jealous, Wrathful, Vengeful kind of Entity continued to be disbursed with the good because of the infiltrations of Jehovah's energies into the mass.

6. It was evident throughout the Heaven Worlds *that another Great One must be sent to erase the scars of fear that had been seeded into the hearts of humanity by the Jehovah energies.* My Children had come to think of me in a way that I am not, to think of My

Ways in a way that I am not. I AM a Loving Father to My Children. I long to see that Love returned to Me. I desire to see their trust in Me. Instead they have been turned away in fear of Me as one who is unapproachable; thus the seeds of separation were sewn and brought forth separation from My people. The Great Divine plan for this Planet evolves around the solution of this complex problem.

7. Therefore, My beloved Firstborn, the Son of Love and Light was commissioned to appear among men to speak to them of Me and My Ways, of My Kingdom, prepared and readied for them and the Love and Great Gifts laid up in store for them for their joy and benefit forever and ever. *HE CAME! He delivered His Message! He planted My SEEDS OF TRUTH and set the old records into proper perspective. He dealt directly with the LOVELESS ONES and there was a gnashing of Teeth for they would not consider their Fallen Thoughts Forms, the perverted encodements of Light, that had been released.* So it was, that they clung still to the old ways, the old words, the old wrongs, AND THEY SLEW HIM WHOM I HAD SENT as they had done My Prophets before Him, and an even greater darkness settled down to envelop the planet.

8. In the quiet places down through the corridors of time, beyond the place where man could see, I still had many of my Great Ones, the ETERNALS, who came and departed in their ambiguity and solitude, behind cloistered walls, hidden in the temples on the mountain tops the shepherds hills in the byways of the Orient, those who mothered the Truth, nurtured it, preserved it while the world sped on in its absorption with the perversion of written words of its scriptures as they called them.

9. These perversions of Truth written for the confusion of mankind have been designed to feed the ongoing fear spawned within human hearts by Jehovah, the Master Deceiver of souls. So it is that in this day this world is covered with religions in abundance that built their castles on the sands of lies from the Great Deceiver. He who has cloned in his likeness the Soulless Ones and sent them forth to enslave mankind in their abominable schemes of destruction of human forms in various and sundry ways, without Love, without Mercy. Yeah even unto the little children now do they ploy their cunning

10. In this hour throughout the kingdom of man, none can buy nor sell except it be within the tentacles of the economic monster

controlled by the Master Mind of Jehovah in his cunning in his worldwide trap placed for mankind. There is no financial group entity nor organization anywhere upon this planet that is not in his clutches and stranglehold grip for coming destruction. For endless times upon times, wars have been staged and waged to feed this gluttony of manipulated world economy and the enslavement of human souls along with the perversion of the destiny of this beautiful planet. THIS SHALL NOT STAND!

Middle East Manipulator
Part 3

1. Now is the time when all things shall be righted. Now is the hour when My son Jehovah shall be given his opportunity to learn the Emotion of Love to return to the Father's House to loosen his death grip upon the sons and daughters of God. I the Father Of All, announce to My Children that *he has now come into your midst.*

2. You are now approaching the most powerful time of your Earth year, vibrationally speaking. Jehovah, in his wisdom knowing this, opted to make his entrance this early before Passover, to avoid the difficulties in negotiating the higher energies being embedded in Earth's atmosphere at this time. It will take him about six months to become acclimated to his embodiment. His age is in the early thirties, fair of form with the strength of youth. Jehovah has entirely overshadowed the entity in the details of its human preparation in earth affairs, for his coming, but the being is in total the energies of Jehovah incarnate.

3. He appears as great shining power that he is, for is he not My son? He comes Into the religious arena of Jerusalem and the Israel race. Many will say, "Now surely we have seen the Christ of God." But as they look for any exemplifying of love in any manner they shall not find it. For love is not in him. He has not experienced that emotion and his incapability of expressing it is his downfall.

4. His battle will be with the Forces of Light, one of control and power. He desires to maintain his control but as he enters into the domain which he has controlled for so long from above, he will realize that it is an entirely different picture than that which he has envisioned. He will face much difficulty attempting to bring forth his kind of power when the truth rests in the Light and Love of the Most

23

High. He will try to discredit all that which is represented by the Light, and therefore he will attack the very nature of peace itself. He instigates a false peace plan which gets the attention of the world. But because of a strong personal power trip, with no love in evidence, he becomes a detriment to his brothers and sisters, manifesting deeds blatantly, not acts of love. He will discredit all of those who choose to display love to their brothers and sisters with even the sex issue a big part of his approach. As we introduce our comments later along on the book of Revelations, we will see the strength and the power of his coming leadership and the volume of his armed services. All eyes will soon be upon the Middle East and his manipulation of events there.

5. I have permitted his entrance into this dimension that he might learn his Great Lesson, for it is here that he shall be exposed to that which will teach him the meaning of love. A woman of great spiritual gifts shall recognize him and announce his presence. She shall exhort him and many will follow her words. She shall bear unto him a son and he shall learn the love of a father for a son. The child he would appear to father is actually being brought forth through the seed of another via his twin flame. She will not of course disclose the truth in this regard and Jehovah will understand only that it is his child. The soul which embodies the child is that of the Father and not of any lessor God. Realize that I cannot permit the seed of Jehovah to be brought forth in any way in these latter days upon the Earth. This seed of confusion has been isolated from the life force of the Father never to appear in the third dimension again.

6. His lesson comes to him when by the hands of his own (Jehovah) followers shall his son be slain. In his sorrow unrequited shall he too be slain by the sword of those of Jehovah. The child will be slain by one who is actually going to be entrusted with the child, not by the midwife as some have said. The difference is that a child of Light will actually be supporting the birthing process of this being and will initially be in charge until such time as one of Jehovah's own takes over. The reason for this fact is so that the father can witness the love energy emitted by the child of Light in contrast to that of his own creation.

7. Though slain by one of his own, Jehovah will be ascended in the process of his death. He will take his form with him as he will

24

have learned to appreciate it in his experience on Earth. In his devastation and sorrow beyond the veil once more he will then learn the lesson of Love, he shall learn the lesson of Grief and the veil of tears shall flood his way, and he shall not partake of deception ever more. He will settle in for so long a term of reflection upon his experience he will gain complete stability and will in all likelihood attempt to replay some of his old scenes of the past. I will not tolerate this nor will the Universe. Though all religions shall have indirectly turned to him with acclaim, he shall know that the purpose for his coming was for his lesson.

8. Many who walk the pathway of discernment in this day shall know his deception and incapability of love. And when My Great One comes who shall bear in His body the mark of the 999 of My Being, those who discern shall know Him of whom I speak. For discernment shall not come from the Teachers, it shall not come from the studies, it shall not come from writings sacred, so called, but it shall come from within. For only there doth the Father abide amongst His Children and He shall whisper unto them the Way, and they shall hear and they shall see and they shall walk therein and they shall not fall prey to these things, for even now they await in the shadows and in the silence the sound of My Footsteps, the breath of My Breath upon them and the end of all these sorrows. I AM THAT I AM HATH SPOKEN WITH THEE.

Father's Intervention
Part 4

1. I AM the Father Mother God, Creator of All That is and ever shall be. It is I who write these words that My Children might come to know the Truth of all Things and be given their opportunity to choose their way.

2. In our last discussion it was with great sorrow on My part, of necessity, thus to so speak concerning one of My sons. However it is the urgency of the times that now comes to the planet that makes My intervention vital to the welfare of All of My Children who abide upon it as well as the urgency for Mother Earth herself. The time that remains for life in your physical dimension grows shorter by he moment. Soon that moment dawns when all things shall have been made right.

3. As I have spoken there has come to the planet in this short interval a visitation of the Jehovah energies. With stature of great beauty, brown hair and fair complexion and eyes of blue to pierce the gaze of his listeners. However Love is not with him, and his words shall reveal that emptiness but in a very clever vein.

4. Much confusion will center around this Great One as he demonstrates his knowledge of the teachings of that which is supported by your Bible. He will not be able to be tricked for his knowledge will be awesome in nature. Know that he will not be able to be beaten intellectually, for this Great One will hold all of the knowledge within his surface mind unlike those who will seek to remove him from their presence.

5. He will be exceedingly keen in the sense of his knowingness and will be capable of knowing the thoughts of others before they speak. This will pose much difficulty when one tries to approach him without the ability to be free of those thoughts which may represent conflict to him. If he is approached with conflict in mind, he will be aware of this long before such an encounter takes place. We mention this because of the necessity of some of My Special Ones having to encounter him before the final days are over. He shall be beaten, but only in the sense of his removal from this planetary region. The ministration of his Great Wisdom shall continue for a very limited time. His defeat shall be his removal from the scene by the hands of his own creations. Nevertheless in the midst of all else that occurs, great chaos will be rempant on all levels of planetary life. None shall scarcely note his withdrawal; such shall be the global disturbances manifesting within My Schedule. It is his leadership that will have released war in the Middle East. He shall return to upper worlds once more, but the chaos of Israel will be in full sway as well as the disasters of Earth.

6. This is not set forth as any attempt to change the thinking of persons nor to dissuade them from their basic tenets of faith in My Person. To those who have known the Father, no deception is possible. Now that the Fallen ones are no longer in access to the Light codes due to come forth upon the planet, these encoded rays of enlightenment shall be recived by humanity in purest form. These words to My Children have been locked in the soul of My Messenger until this proper time had come for their release.

7. So all must think for themselves and remain open in their discernment of My Words. This is not presented for judgment, but rather for discernment within the knowingness of the Light that now comes to Creation in this generation. Now the presence of My *Spiritual Israel,* collectively reflecting their light within this setting of the stage, so to speak, now do I dare to lift the veil to expose the Great Deception, the heartbreaking hoax that has been perpetuated upon My Children in these many cycles of time. In our next conversation, I will lead you through perversions of the last book of your Bible and others that pertain so closely to the days upon us. I AM the Father. My Love is ever with All of you.

Stroke of Diabolical Genius
Part 5

1. I AM THAT I AM, THE FATHER, I come to continue our conversations for the writing of words for My Children.

2. With the removal of My Beloved Son from the Earth scene and those sent with Him to surround and support his Mission, the stage was made ready for yet a Greater Deception. The New Testament of his words was to have represented a New Agreement between Me and My Children: a New Covenant between us to replace the old corruption and destruction of the false separation from My Children of All races.

3. The preparation and the compiling of the documents beckons the most fertile ground Jehovah had ever controlled for his distorted purposes. Further, to insure that all Harmony and Unity would be totally erased from My Divine Plan, letters or writings from the Helper Souls (Apostles) were inserted into the Holy Collection and henceforth ascribed to be My Words. Out of these, all divisions, all disunity and human burdens hard to be born would come upon My Children. But the pure, simple etchings of My Son were obscured in generations of human commentaries. His words were Light and did not require interpretation when spoken to the people for they were My Truth sent to My sons and daughters. They will now be greatly interested to see just how this further Deception was injected into the minds of mankind. The Deception was assured of timeless success when the distortion was elevated to that position of being the only criteria confused man might use to measure the valid-

ity of all future revelation! Thus did My Children turn from Me to worship not a Golden Calf at this time, but an object of their own creation. Therefore a way out of the Great Deception it was thought would never be found.

4. This was Jehovah master stroke of Genius, preparing the foundation for the coming great separations and great divisions of My Children. But is he not a God? Is he not My son, a true prince of Divine royalty. Indeed he is rightly called The Prince of this world and *not* another whom you call by another name.

5. I would request My Daughter, that you would follow my words as together we venture into the last book of that volume which your world terms its Holy Bible. Time now approaches so closely to those days described therein we must now quickly release this information for the benefit of My Children upon whom this clever deceiver shall focus his attention.

6. We shall explore this portion of the writings to set straight many things that for endless centuries have been permitted acceptance as they stand, unaware of the polluted influence previously prepared for just such a time as this. In My Kingdom. The loveless force has set the stage for eons of time designed for performance at this apocalyptic hour.

7. Those who have followed the many perversions of these Revelations shall continue in total confusion. It was a true rendering by him who received it. It was, however, the further interpolations of other hands and minds that rearranged and restated the body of the discussions, until that which went forth was a total departure from the original vision and words in commentary, even in sequence. Some isolated portions considered irrelevant at the time have escaped manipulation while other portions were grossly reversed in their final rendering. In the days ahead, together we must search out those portions of Light as well as those of human contrivance to set straight the record before the coming of the desolation in Jerusalem takes place. In tomorrow's discussion we shall begin this unveiling. Perhaps My Children should read with Bible in hand. I shall continue tomorrow.

Section 2

Getting It Right

"Love Letters From The Throne"

My children, I have long awaited these end times, as you refer to them, for this most precious planet. I have sorrowed much over the travesties of this planetary experience. Mother Earth has been shedding many tears over the many eons of time, time that she has made Herself available for this expression of creation.

She so desires for these end times to be completed that her sorrow radiates back to Me, with what you might consider much pain. I too am pleased about that which is to follow in terms of her release from this pain.

I, too, desire all of mankind to understand that which is to come to pass. I, too, want all of mankind to understand the meaning of this pain which the planet has withstood for so long in order that mankind could play out its fantasies. NOW WE MUST ALL MOVE ON.

I have called and commissioned you to proceed forward with your work, establishing the end occurrences as they must come according to the grand plan. I have asked that you go forward to cleansing from this planet that which she desires to have removed from her. We have asked that you have a consciousness of those who have chosen their own will over Mine, and that you have a sense of their right place.

I so care for all My children that I have prepared a home for even those who reject My Presence in their life experiences. I am of course saddened by their unwillingness to accept that I am the Father, but this is fine, as they most certainly will desire My Presence once they have lived any length of time in the darkness. I am sorrowful that this has to come to pass....but so be it.

You, My loving Ones, will be graciously received at My table as the Feast is now being prepared. I have made great plans for this Celebration and will not rest not a day until this Feast comes to pass. I give My Thanks to you, for your devotion to My plan for that which you call planet Earth. I have been grateful for all that you have done and welcome you home when that time comes. I remain with you always. Your loving Father/Mother God.

• • •

The Holy 999
Part 6

1. I AM THE FATHER OF ALL CREATION. I AM THE BEGINNING AND THE END, THE ALPHA AND OMEGA OF ALL THAT IS AND EVER SHALL BE. I CONTINUE NOW IN OUR CONVERSATIONS FOR THE BENEFIT OF MY CHILDREN EVERYWHERE.

2. The studies and deductions along with the discussions of My Sons Jesus and Michael with you have been most interesting to Me. These various questions in your mind truly represent the motivation present in this work we do. This portion of the named Holy Book is so riddled with these errors under discussion, there barely remains enough time to unravel them.

3. You have finally located in your search the *only passage or use of the number 666* in the entire written record. In vain did you search for another, for no other corresponding witness exists anywhere. For it is here at this point in the record (Rev. 13:18) that the perversion of this number made entry, calculated and deliberate in its destructive intent. In the (four) references to this subject that follow, the number becomes a mark that is *not My Seal*. The few references that follow go on to expand the prized lie that it is the "mark of the beast" and even that it appears in the forehead as well as the hand. Once an awareness is born of these interferences and the motive, the entire proposal is clearly exposed.

4. The number 999 is identified as truly of My Kingdom. It represents a Divine number of the Creation of Life itself in this and other Universes. This is a widely known fact in other worlds. It is a code number within the consciousness of many who have come to

31

this planet to serve the Father, and who are actual extensions of My Self. To disguise this number as a mark of the Fallen ones has diabolically and thoroughly confused the souls of this planet, but it was easily accomplished by another source simply by inverting the number upside down.

5. My Daughter, there is a great need for Us to unfold this story, to surface it in human minds to assist with the mass confusion which will surface regardless. So many have long waited the fulfillment of the prophecy concerning the mark of the beast. I have made provisions for this lesson to come forth. It is unfortunate that the lesson will be played out to the detriment of those who have changed its meaning and representation. For this is actually the mark of the Great Eternal Ones and not that of the Fallen Ones. This distortion will play havoc for those without proper intunement within and for whom discernment is outside their personal experience. It will be denounced by religious zealots who are programmed to biblical writings but without soul discernment. The confusion soon to follow for My Children will be of such abnormality many will be prevented from moving into higher realms of expression.

6. Numbers are identities used widely in the upper realms. Even worlds, planets, are coded by number and not by name upon the great monitoring boards of My Flying Brotherhood. Yes 999 is the number of a man as written, but it is not as originally written. The number was written by, recorded by, another who feigned the mind and thought of the Messenger. Beyond that time there were many other rewritings of the words and many versions with opportunities for revision. At the time, there existed strong sensitivity to the existence of an army of darkness with its certain great leader, whom they chose to call Satan. The system was formulated and elaborated upon by the priests and scribes of this Devil, out of their intense desire to have control of the people in their influence upon them. Ignorance and bigotry fueled the plan. For endless centuries My People did not have access to this written transcription nor the spirituality to receive for themselves. The record remained unchallenged. Only the priesthood had access to the holy writings and to the possibility of changing them as they desired. In the earliest centuries of the church, the writings were tampered with to imply that the mark was of a negative application and an identity of those of darkness.

7. I ask My Light Workers to realize that neither the dark ones nor the Fallen ones need an identifying mark, because they cannot hide themselves nor their ways from the discerning Child of Light. It is indeed by their works that ye know them.

8. Three identifying insignias are engraved within My Children: in the heart, the flame of Love; in the membrane of the hand, the number of Creation; in the head, the shining morning star. It has been written that without the mark of the beast, neither shall any man buy nor sell. This is consistent with that which has been given, for the nines of My Kingdom will not be involved in the buy and sell for their needs, for money will cease to exist. One's wants and needs shall be provided by My Hand as is proper, so that buying and selling will fade away in the new scheme of things. The plan of the Fallen ones to thus make a degenerated mark upon My Children was an ingenious one. For now in the closing days as I prepare to lift the veil, there is the sad possibility of misjudgment of the Light.

9. Therefore I call upon My Enlightened Teachers to bring forth this exposure in time for end time events. Some uninformed Lighted Ones will even classify the exposure itself as being of the Fallen ones but My Sons Michael and the Beloved One are with you to guide you through the jungle of human opinion. There will be no more martyrs. The plan has been set aside. No more blood shall be shed for Truth. Man has Truth on his own hands from this time forward; it will not dissolve by removing its source.

10. When this My revelation concerning the number 999 goes forth, it will be the Bible worshippers who will bring the fiercest opposition and not the Light Workers or My volunteers of these times. The crystallization of this concept is so embedded within souls that there will be no hope of delivering them from it as long as they cling to the old thought forms. The sense of Satan is an indoctrination that spans too many centuries of time. It is even more solidified than the concept of the substitutionary scapegoat atonement of My Son. In too many movements only an entirely new incarnation will accomplish the removal of these perversions of My Divine Plan.

11. I state once again, though I repeat my words, this sacred number is used throughout My Kingdom to identify My Creation. It does NOT designate those who are not of the Light. Only those who carry this insignia are able to enter into the higher realms. They are capable because they have earned this mark. No mark exists for those who have not earned the right to enter. I AM determined to shed Light upon this error in biblical presentation concerning the number 666. This heavenly number is placed within the membrane in order that it be preserved for the entire incarnation. Without it, those who would desire to evolve into the higher realms would not be enabled to do so. This distortion was created within the inner realms because the dark forces would like those identified with the mark of God, to be removed by the lessor forces of their making. Thus they would like it to be believed that the mark represents the beast when in fact the beast is already known to be that of the dark forces themselves. The beast needs no further identification, for his presence is obvious in all that is not of the Light. I AM the Father of My Creation. I will not ever allow My Children to be branded in any physical way. This is not within the consciousness of mankind and it shall not come to pass. It will be known that this holy number (666-999) is of My Making, in identifying My Children, throughout My Kingdom.

12. This is the number of those who will be entering into the ninth dimension after their mission is over. It is a most unusual number in the sense that it cannot be reversed in any way. It is that which it is. The fact that it is presented upside down is another way of identifying the touch of the dark forces upon it. The number 666–999 is only for those who are of the highest evolved state, who if taken out of their mission would not be able to support the transformation process and thereby would leave without completing the mission. The dark forces would have no problems ruling over this planet if they could remove those who bear this number as prescribed in the biblical record. The reversal of the number has no significance whatsoever in the higher realms. The number always equates to nine however it is facing. This will be the code that will be exposed, for the number nine is the highest level of completion before entering into the dimension of total spirit, at which point numbers become another part of the being itself. Numbers are then no longer necessary for understanding the Universe when passed beyond all dimensions. The reason that thorough understanding of this distortion is so vital is that *in the final days there will be many who are capable of seeing this marking in those who walk in great Light. Without*

knowledge, the marking will therefore create the potential for those
capable of seeing it, to dismiss that Light Worker as being of the
dark ones. Therefore the dark forces pit the LIGHT AGAINST THE
LIGHT and bring forth in depth confusion. Remember, the dark
ones do not have a numerical reference so it is not necessary to eval-
uate any number within their being.

13. But My concern for My Loving Children goes beyond number. It also carries with it *the Codings* to bring forth the true identity
of the Light Worker. As long as there remains distortion in understanding this, there will be a distortion in the awakening of that one
seeking the Light. This is why the Dark Forces were prone to make
this a part of the puzzle of prophecy which would further complicate
the understanding of those in the Light, as well as those who would
be grounded in the distortion, and not in the understanding of the
higher truths.

14. I welcome My Children to seek My Face and listen for My
Voice to bring forth from within their own being a clearer understanding of all of these things. The Father hath spoken with you.

Anti Christ? Father's Reply
Part 7

1. I AM the Father Mother Creator, of All that is, to continue
our conversations to be shared with My Children.

2. As we penetrate deeply into the errors that have been placed
with humanity, I desire at this time to discuss the Being termed in
your scriptures as Lucifer. Because of Jehovah's intent to distort all
Truth, it naturally follows that he would carefully plot to defame the
Highest of My Shining Angels. With the attention of the religious
world upon his perverted words, he took One of the Great Ones,
The Eternal Being of Light, and named him Lucifer and made him to
be a being of darkness and a vessel of evil.

3. Lucifer is the Angel of Light, the Morning Star, and is not,
nor will he ever be anything else. Lucifer has embodied upon Earth
many times to support My Plan and to offset the forces brought
forth by Jehovah. Why then would Jehovah not choose to show My
Son Lucifer as one of the Fallen ones when in fact he is not.

4. The number 666 (999) is that of Lucifer certainly, but it is
Lucifer who comes to save the planet from the destructive forces of

Jehovah. The Dark Ones took the highest of the number of the Universe, the Holy 999, and reversed its posture and gave the number into this demented character of defied evil and called him Devil. This sacred number, which is embedded within every Lighted Being, Jehovah perverted to mean the number of this Imaginary Devil. We of the Universal Creative Forces do not need to number the Fallen ones to identify them, for they are exposed for all to see and are known to all men. We DO number our Angels and Beings of Enlightenment with the Sacred number of Light, 999 which *remains 9 regardless of how the number is manipulated or broken (6+6+6=18=9; 9+9+9=28=9) 999 is the number of My Saints, the number of My Kingdom, and the Glorious New Earth.* THERE IS NO BEAST, THERE IS NO DEVIL, THERE IS NO ANTI-CHRIST FOR CHRIST FORCE DOES NOT NEED AN OPPOSITE.

5. Lucifer, so called, a beloved son, has come to Earth by many names, but the names are not important here. What is important is that he bears MY Standard of Light and Truth, to advance Harmony and Balance within humanity.

6. It is My Will at this time, that the secret of this "mark" or number be released. It has been kept from My Children when they have accepted words that have no truth. Each energy force projected from the Source represents a mathematical relationship to Me, summarized in a number. This mark of which we speak is one such energy which has been projected. It will be obvious and clear to those who know this mark who it is that is carrying it within his genetic makeup, and clear to all of those who see. It will surface within the minds of Light Workers, for they will know that it is I who comes to them with this mark. There will be a clear knowingness that the mark of 999 (666) resides within this individual. The confusion will arise as a result of this Being representing himself as one who comes in the Name of My Energies.

7. Do not confuse this as any reference to an Anti-Christ. THERE IS NO SUCH THING. This representation in the biblical sense was trying to refer to the Fallen One who was instrumental in setting up this process whereby polarities could be experienced. As a result of this misunderstanding the Anti-Christ concept came into being in terms of one's attempt to understand events in heaven worlds. The Anti-Christ was proposed to be the opposite of Christ,

but Christ has no opposite, understand this! THE LIGHT DOES NOT NEED THE DARKNESS NOR DOES LOVE NEED AN OPPOSITE IN ORDER TO BE.

8. So much misunderstanding has prevailed through many ages with biblical teachings to foster control of mankind within the context of socalled religious freedom. The compiling of its contents was intentionally designed to *limit the understanding of the followers. For if man knew, the church following would be limited to only those incapable of accepting truth, not of the Light so to speak.*

9. Religion has resulted in the accumulation of money in centers for the benefit of their leaders and their desire for power/control in MY Name. The false truth structure they have used will crumble with them. The Eternal One who returns to the scene to make all things right will himself be accused of being the Beast for he will clearly represent the number of his essence in full light of day. As his perfection comes to the surface the gnashing of teeth concerning the mark will be all that religions will have to cling to. THAT IS WHY IT IS SO IMPERATIVE, URGENT, THAT WE PRESENT INFORMATION AT THIS TIME, FOR THE MOMENT OF RECKONING IS FAST APPROACHING MY CHILDREN.

10. My purpose for revealing 666 is to present to humanity another opportunity for total awakening and an opportunity to Know Me as a Heavenly Father who Loves and Cares for them all.

Removal of the Fallen Ones
Part 8

1. I AM THAT I AM speaks with thee, to continue our conversations to be given to MY children as they prepare themselves for the events of My schedule.

2. "My endtime revelations could not have been released before this time. The energies were not present to grasp them, as they are now. The response from Our readers is gratifying and proves the stirring within hearts that has been created. This is My intention: to wake up souls, to focus their attention and get them thinking, arguing, opposing or whatever it takes to maintain that attention to be drawn to My Words, My Truth. I care not what they say but I care that they will read and respond and talk, with an interchange that is an evidence of Life! *Only the corpse is still and silent.* And so My

Child, do not consider that this thing we do is a small thing, for it is not. IT IS A POWERFUL TIME FOR MY POWERFUL WORDS TO BE GIVEN TO THIS GENERATION: words which will decode the inner levels of their Being.

3. We must work together to bring to My Seed upon this planet, an understanding of things to come; as these have been scheduled by Me for the punctuating of the last days when the fallen ones shall hold sway in this place which they have trespassed and usurped these myriad eons of cycles and times that are past.

4. I AM therefore directing the ministry of your focused energies, at that time appointed by Me and My Emissaries of Light, to cover every mile of the western coastline of this country from tip to tip, to expel in Divine ritual, the presence of fallen ones from that important portal of Earth.

5. It may always be assumed that all events occur on three levels simultaneously: physically, mentally and spiritually. The vehicles of your physical forms act as transformers to all of the environment around you when you are on any special mission. In this case there will not only be the intervening rays of the Hierarchical energies, but there will be the explosions of electromagnetic help coming into you from the fleets above. As the calls are given and as your forms travel through an area, these magnetic beams will be beamed out from the ships throughout the areas for the 100 mile radius in all directions.

6. At the moment of the call, thousands of fallen ones will gather around you and be escorted by the angels and the fleets to their destination. A call will go forth that this opportunity will be given, and believe me dear one, there are many even now, who anxiously await this opportunity for a peaceful departure, knowing their time to do so has come. The Angels will hold back and away from that radius, any whose intent is negative of nature to the plan or to your persons. This protective honor guard will be accompanying you every mile of the way, regardless of what the physical plane activity might be. This is a journey which we will all partake of. Following the rituals, the places of solitude, a response may be received as to the results of details of that particular ceremony.

7. In every hundred miles you shall pause and do this thing, that My Divine Emissaries may minister through your words and your form to the Mother, and they shall gather to them and remove all of

those ones that shall answer that command to remove to their place.

8. It is not within My Heart or My Plan that any tiniest portion of this beautiful coastline shall fall away from reality but that it shall be preserved for the great mission and destiny that awaits this Planet. It is My Divine Will to preserve intact this area of Great Light. Therefore I send you to this place on this special mission, accompanied by My Great Host, dedicated to the final cleansing of earth, who will overshadow, guide and assist this action from the skies above you, as I have requested.

9. I send you also, to cover in like manner, the coastlines of the country of Mexico, this sacred land so special to Our Beloved Mary. This ritual of removing the fallen ones through interaction of several dimensions, anchored through your energies, is of great importance to the final segments of My Plan which I shall bring forth at a later writing.

10. Other cleansings of the Planet will take place in many different manner of events within My Schedule and overshadowing of circumstances. But the removal of the fallen ones, now clustered so densely in your midst, is a basic action that clears the way for other successive measures to follow. Their presence increases the turmoil for humanity. You are Commissioned and Empowered to speak directly and with destroyers and your voice will carry the Authority of My Decree and this shall be known by them.

11. The American continents are the Great Baskets of My harvest to magnetized the Light, to contain My Will, and Cradle My Children for Earth's Destiny. I speak of a mystery, but the mystery shall soon be revealed, for not many know of My Plans for this body of Creation but I shall make it known to them.

The Issue of Prophesy by "The Father"

12. I am with you my children and I too can only reveal that which is known as a result of all that has been accumulated in what is known to you as the Universal Mind. I am all knowing, but that all knowingness does not extend to that which has never been known.

13. I want you to know that your perception of I, the All Knowing Father, is correct, it is just that one must realize that if all knowledge existed now, there would be no reason to explore within My being that which has yet to surface in what you refer to as "knowl-

edge." There is a great misperception about past, present and future. It is true that they are all one in the Universal NOW, but with the moment of eternity lies a vast degree of opportunity to experience and create. When I first projected the First Born it was unknown at that time what this activity would lead to. Even though there was an opportunity to know, it had to be experienced before that knowledge became one with the totality of consciousness which you often refer to as Me.

14. I will tell you that which is within the Universal Mind based on all known factors of creation at this time. What remains unknown even within My consciousness is the full extent of the nature of how "will" creatures react to the coming events. Let us take a simple example. Many have committed to serve in My name on your planet Earth. Many have stepped forth from this Throne through numerous ways to lead the forces of creation into new walks of life. Many have made claims to others of what they are capable of doing and yet as you know many have fallen short of that which they set forth to do. This is not a judgement but the facts of the matters which were involved with these episodes of creation. Now we have a solution involving earth which has NEVER ever happened in the history of all the known Universe. This sequence which we will go through together is going to be based only on that which is perceivable by My Presence that resides in all creation. Does this help?

15. Prophesy is not always brought forth from the Throne. Many prophets were up against the same things that you are currently involved with. First, you have limits of understanding in your use of linear concepts. Second, you as a collective consciousness within earth, have been cut off from the direct projections from My Throne; much can get distorted in the process. Third, you have been under the influence of those, who some of my children refer to as the fallen ones (who are by the way also of my origin). Those who have opted to follow a plan that was not in harmony with All of creation have allowed certain processes to take place that have clearly distorted the pathways to truth. In addition, prophesy is brought forth to allow the consciousness of the entity, to which it is revealed, to raise his consciousness to a higher level in order to prevent those things which can be prevented. Some prophesy of course cannot be prevented within the lower realms of creation. From higher realms, most if not all prophesy can be altered by the forces that are contained within My Being.

16. The medium must be clear in order to bring forth those concepts which are only involved with the highest truths and then to put them into linear concepts known to you as words.

17. I know My children how precious you are in your commitment to those words which have been assembled in your Bible but this is not the total source of knowledge nor is the written word from that which you know as I the Creator. All who brought forth this information did so within third dimensional consciousness even though many had the abilities to reveal the greater truths. The third dimension is even limiting for the Great Ones. In addition to the difficulties to bring forth the WORD as you know it, there was desire on the part of the fallen ones to change many words through extraction of material and direct alterations. It is not necessary to get stuck in the past but what is important is to clear the way within your own consciousness to be set free, as my Son Jesus has said many times.

18. Some Bible prophesies tie directly to the cosmic clock and cannot be altered. Others are clearly in the hands of the mass consciousness and can be affected by right thought.

19. They are records of energy movements at the time that the prophesies were brought forth. Why do you believe that prophesy is brought forth? It is a tool for change. Are there not lessons to be learned in the moment that it is delivered that could be forsaken when time comes to pass?

20. You must understand why Jesus brought forth that which he did in terms of prophesy. It represented the codes to the future based on the momentums of the present. Had certain activities not been averted, (example—World War II) there would be more prophesy actualized.

21. That was the war capable of ending the planet as we know it and would have been that which fulfilled future prophesy. That was not the final Armeggedon as this is still going to happen in the Middle East. What World War II did represent was the state of man's consciousness which reflected upon what would have taken place in the future had certain Intervention not taken place. It was determined in the higher realms that enough was enough.

22. Names are not the issue. ANYTIME ONE TRIES TO

LABEL MY PRESENCE THEN THEY WILL LIMIT THEIR OWN PERSPECTIVE OF MY BEING. Do not try to EXPRESS ALL WITH THE NAMES that have been brought forth into earth's consciousness for once again you will spend your time concerned about that which is not relevant to one's mission of Light. Many have come in My name bringing forth that which they perceived as being truth. The truth however does not come from sources external BUT FROM WITHIN. No matter who the middle man is, it will limit ones view of truth by trying to restrict truth to words and words to actions. TAKE ACTION FROM THE TRUTH THAT RESIDES WITHIN and you can set yourself free from words written in books, which as I have stated, will limit your ability to do the mission which you were called forth to do.

23. All came from within. If you chose to use a source, be it any source, you need merely use your own discernment. NO ONE NEEDS TO HOLD TO THAT WHICH WAS BROUGHT FORTH OUTSIDE OF HIMSELF. Once you move outside the limited consciousness resulting from the veil over the planet you will reside in the truth and become one with it. You then are beyond words, beyond the Bible and beyond all non-harmonious thoughts of one's own personal perceptions.

24. Prophesy can only lead one in the DIRECTION of My Presence. YOU CAN ONLY FIND ME WITHIN and this is the message that is the only message of truth that you can comprehend in earth languages. All teachings say this no matter what language. No matter what the words represent THIS IS THE TRUTH WHICH SETS MAN FREE FROM LIMITATION and is ALL THAT I AM PERSONALLY CONCERNED with.

25. Prophesy is a tool. If it was not meant to be a tool then it would have no benefit to those to whom the words were meant. I am a loving Father above all else and would have liked all of mankind to reach out to Me to change the events which were within man's ability. This was and has not been the case when prophesy has been revealed however, mainly due to the various ego constraints involved in creatures of will.

26. You are that which makes history. You are the prophet of today, and tomorrow you perhaps will be written about as being a great prophet. Who are these great prophets but none other than

aspects of creation itself. I wish you to know how important you are in the creative experience of Mother Earth. Do not reduce yourself to past tense or to someone who has not the power of creative expression that could alter the course of events that other aspects of yourself brought forth many years ago. I AM the Father who speaks in Love to all of you.

Section 3

The Father's Schedule

Looking Toward the Middle East

1. As winter approaches be alert for the surfacing of a leadership in Israel of great cunning: one who will accrue a tremendous following in shortness of time. A contagious but diabolical enthusiasm will fill the coming year with full scaled warfare contained within that which is called the Holy Land. World governments will focus alarmed attention upon this phenomena. By those days Gorbachev will have his government in hand with full cooperation from his staff of leaders.

2. Great China will have a new leader positioned in agreement with the political demands current to the protests of the hour. Israel will have its new leader fast gaining unofficial power with the people and leading them into Atomic war against their Arab brothers. The hostilities will continue unabated for perhaps a year with no international body able to successfully intervene in any manner. The coming of Wormwood could be the final intervention of this great sorrow."

3. It is when Israeli forces introduce Atomic weaponry that *the days of the still wind* will begin. Then My Four Mighty Angels shall hold back the four winds of the Earth that they may not blow upon the Earth nor on the sea nor on any tree. *(Re 7:1)* For it is not to be that other parts of Creation shall suffer from the intent of My son Jehovah to destroy his neighbors with Atomic energies. It is ordained in heaven worlds that this conflict shall not now engage an entire world but shall be contained in that area of its karmic destiny.

4. Therefore its destruction that falleth at noonday shall fall only upon those who have chosen to experience it. Therefore shall not My winds move forth this plague to the dwellings of My Seed

45

elsewhere *(localized atomic war—T)*. Whatever activity or circumstance or need which is requiring of the wind will suffer to be without it. Your flags shall hang limp, your boats remain motionless. Pollution will be oppressive in your cities. The ministry of My Two Witnesses in Jerusalem will close off the rainfall that it rain not in the days of their Prophecy. *(Re 11)*.

5. There will be no manner to cleanse the air or the atmosphere as is with you now. The blanket of Pollution will prevail but it will hold back that which falleth from the middle east insanities. Your conditioning of the air will be a necessity and the density belched forth from your vehicles and manufacturing localities will need to be halted in their actions The inability of persons to go outside of their homes will compound economical crises as well. These days of the stilling of the winds are the days when the very atmosphere could burn due to the many gasses displacing it with no relief from nature.

6. When nuclear fallout is passed, the winds will be released to blow again. With the ascension of the Witnesses, the rains will fall again and it will be safe to breathe once more. My hurricanes of wind and rains are upsetting and of course disturbing to human life, but consider that these do leave in their wake air that is purified and cleansed once more where the winds and rains have been. The greenery of your growing things adds to the quality of your air. Preserve these agents of life.

144,000 Special Emissaries
Part 10

1. The next two years will encompass many different lessons for mankind but for the most part it will be a time of final preparations for Mother Earth. The Eternal Ones are very much involved in this process. In the past I have permitted My Sons, the LORDS OF LIGHT, to move the schedule around in accordance with My Will, but this is no longer possible. I have now brought forth My schedule of events for these last days. My earth-based special ones know that which they must do as well as those in the higher realms who are all aware of this schedule and have made their final preparations in accordance to their specific roles.

2. These are the days when My 144,000 Great Ones are with you for this great finale, these who have repeatedly served as My

Emissaries and volunteers to the Blessed Mother Earth. They are representative of 12 eternal energies or 12 Light rays of Celestia who have also once been with the 12 tribes of Israel in embodiment for those times. They are the Elect who have chosen to maintain responsibility over this entire earth project. They are mostly all now embodied on the planet, those that have chosen to stay with this latter phase of the transition. They are the spiritual Israel but of course are not of any certain human race. They are now sealed with the vibratory patterns necessary for reinstating the Divine Harmonics for Mother. They are present for specific guidance through your cataclysms (earthquakes etc) darkness (ecilpses); collision of worlds; to bring you "out of tribulation" and into the "arks of safety" *(Re 7:14)*. For then will be complete chaos and not requiring of My Light workers who will have their missions complete or aborted.

3. Take care not to confuse in your thinking the Light Workers with the 144,000 Great Ones or planetary volunteers. On this much confusion prevails. Lighted ones may be here to master certain lessons; to awaken; to learn; to grow; to assist perchance to serve with the commissioned ones. But their great multitude *be not the Eternal Emissaries,* projections from My Throne, martyrs for My Truth. Be that which you are and strive not to label thyself what thou art not: for all are My Children. All are provided for in My Kingdom and encircled by My Love.

4. The pervading turmoil that results from the Jerusalem ministry of My Two Witnesses calls forth the massive evacuation of the Lighted Ones because of final cleansing events that immediately explode as the Second Woe is passed and the Third Woe must begin its work *(Re 11:14)*.

5. The lifting away of Light Workers does not empty the planet in one sweep as some in error have given. Special Emissaries remain for their unglamourous work of stabilizing the Earth. These will be the most highly and Divinely protected persons who have ever walked upon Terra. Unawakened Lighted ones who have resisted My Truth and attacked those whom I have sent while refusing their call. must remain for another chance to choose.

6. The greater majority remain beyond that moment still to wallow in their denials of Me as their Creator, caring not to call upon Me even in that hour. The masses will choose to succumb to

their torment before they will humble their pride to call their Heavenly Father. They will simply leave their bodies with the planet as they are overcome by the final cleansing events. They will return to the astral from which they have come. There they will remain until the Angels come to escort then to the place which is prepared for them, *but they will never stand upon this beautiful world again.* Thus it shall be. For the temporary closing down of this planetary activity shall be not only for the healing of Mother, but for the graduation and separation of souls.

7. There is much sorrow within My Being that the unrepentant ones refuse to learn their lessons and thus to progress, but in their separation they can bring no hurt nor heartache to others. My Plan of Love has born no fruit for them yet I have provided for these. The impenitent must ever remember there is ever present My forgiveness in grace and Love until that great gulf of separation becomes their new reality *(Re 16:26).*

Days of the Seventh Seal
Part 11

1. 144,000 Eternal Ones are prepared and trained to stand in the days of the seventh seal. Whether or not they shall remain is subject to their will and choice. My Heart understands the motivation of those who are tired and battle weary; the many will choose to depart to return immediately to other dimensional form to carry on. Yet thousands of other stalwart warriors will remain in their place by covenant: through the sounding of the four trumpets when hail and fire destroys one third of the trees and green growing things and the atmosphere burns. When the roar of the erupting mountains flow their spoil into the waters to contaminate one third of them one third of their sea life and one third of the ships at sea.

2. The Great Ones shall hold the course of Terra when later the Falling Star *(Wormwood)* shall touch the ocean waters, removing many and cutting a pathway through the Solar System to darken a third of the Light from the heaven worlds and blacken four hours of the day and four hours of the night when one third of the Sun and the Moon shall not reveal their Light. The event of the Falling Star ushers in a broad furthering of the consciousness of man especially those unawakened Lighted Ones. For many have been called but few

48

have listened. This is the most sorrowful reality for all of Us, for we know how small the Final Harvest will be. We can only hope that human consciousness will be raised very soon to a level to get many off the fence of doubt and procrastination. I desire to have them all return to My Presence.

3. When the 5th trumpet gives its sound *(Re 9:1–10)* the war of Jehovah begins the First Woe of mankind. The Eternal Ones must hold intact the Light for the planet as this incarnated powerful Leader opens limited atomic war against his brothers using nuclear bomber attacks for five months of time; resulting in consequence of heavy nuclear fallout inversion upon the land. By the stilling of the winds *(Re 7:1)* the contamination is locked in by My Hand and not permitted to drift to those places and nations of My Light.

4. My children must realize at this point in our conversation we are still speaking of the energies of the seventh seal when the Second Woe of humanity takes place and the Angel of the Sixth trumpet sounds *(Re 9:11–17)*. Jehovah now fully releases his forces of 200,000 on land and in the air the bomber fleets. By their action in this acceleration one third of humanity is destroyed yet no remorse is forthcoming from those who have projected this evil.

5. The war has already begun but not of the totality that has been envisioned. The planetary mass that comes forth will not bring an end to this war as it will not end until the cleansing process has been completed. Remember that the territorial battle is over that point on the planet which must be controlled by the fallen ones. If they are to sustain their energies on this planet.

6. You must understand the way of the fallen ones. They distort the truth enough to change the course of history.

7. What is actually going to happen is that man will continue to reject the Presence of God and by doing so will increase karma upon the planet. This will then cause the imbalances that will play themselves out in war, plagues and so on. We monitor these events in order to determine at what point man needs to be saved.

8. Without some degree of accuracy man will not be able to complete his own evolutionary cycle. In other words, if man is freed from the planet too soon many will have to live out their remaining physical lives on planets where beauty and life is not as abundant. This will not be pleasant. If man is left on planet earth too long,

49

karma may build to such an extent that the planet will be unable to handle it.

9. The conflict in Jerusalem is supported by the fallen ones to divert attention from their true purpose of maintaining control of this physical domain. They are all in conflict for control of this most important power center of the planet. It represents HIGH GROUND for planetary dominance therefore it MUST be kept in the Light.

10. The city of Jerusalem will be in a state of siege for at least six months while two of My most Powerful Messengers begin their final mission of holding My Light and Truth as a balancing force against the energies of Jehovah the mighty one, boldly in word and deed in great power and mighty miracles *(Re 11:2–12)*. These shall be slain by the Leaders and their physical forms abandoned in the streets for three and a half days. A boisterous citywide celebration will blaspheme My Words and Deeds through these My Witnesses but on the fourth day My Annointed Ones shall demonstrate their Ascension in sight of all who jeer these things.

11. The clearing out of the fallen ones in the middle east will convince all of the dark ones that their days are over on this planet. They will clear themselves out in most cases but this great demonstration will complete the harvest. All of My Children should properly attune to this event. It is the signal to awaken or to sleep again on a third dimensional platform. Those who walk the line will either turn to Me or deny their own Divine Birthright .

The Final Cleansing
Part 12

1. At that very hour *(Re 11:13)*. My just reward shall shake that city severely taking seven thousand lives bringing widespread repentance and regrets in that place. Most of the children of darkness will continue to worship the Butcher whom their mighty leader has sponsored and a second leader shall set up a world wide closed economic system of monetary slavery *(Re 13:16, 17)*."

2. Then shall there come to them the seven last Plagues *(Re 15:5–8, 16:1–21)* of skin eruptions; sea waters as blood; rivers and waterfalls of crimson red; with ozone layer totally damaged, the Sun will become a scorching fire; the city will abide in darkness and nuclear disease; the past three and a half years of drought will dry

the Euphrates preparing an open path for invasion; and the mightiest earthquake in the history of the planet shall come. The city will be cut into three parts; other cities and islands will vanish. Mountains will collapse. Then shall My Angels release a devastating bombardment of bucket sized hail stones crushing all things beneath the weight of them. Then shall I look upon *(Re 18)* the fall and total destruction of that city of Jerusalem where all of My Prophets have been slain.

3. When the voice of the seven thunders shall begin to speak they shall declare to My Creation that the Mysteries of My Word are finished, that My Kingdom is established, that the end and the fullness of time has come with the completion of the Divine Plan for Earth. There will be no more secrets no more mysteries, all Truth will be laid bare so those of Mine who must find it will find it and the hidden secrets of My Little Book *(Re 10)* which My Son John was requested to withhold.

4. Now My Eternal Ones will reveal the Truth about the Bible lies and the great deception. I am saddened by the extreme confusion to be experienced by My Seed who follow the doctrines of earth religion. I shall overshadow them as they are challenged in understanding with an all knowingness to prepare for their Ascension.

5. As it was in the days of Noah, so the world goes happily forward in its complacency and certainty that the world as it is will continue forever. This is a sad thing, for so very few are prepared in their minds and hearts for the great changes that are before humanity.

6. The Earth Mother can scarcely contain the suffering endured at the hands of destructive mankind: the abominations against Creation itself. Grace and Time are not Limitless. My Grace has its point of Limit and My Promises to Mother Earth must be redeemed. Man's residence upon Earth has been conditional to certain great Principles and Responsibility and Laws of Accountability. There is a distant point in the past when it began and there is a coming point in the now when it will end. Graduation will close Earth's school rooms and the laggards will be released to roam new frontiers of desolation.

7. Heaven cannot make man's decisions: the privilege of choice is the crowning birthright of His embodiment. But My Patience is

not limitless in the amount of suffering I will permit to touch the innocent and the pure in heart.

8. The great experiment of human Creation has ended. The bells are ringing to call My Own to come Home to the Father's House. So many have wandered so far, for so long. Few there will be who will care to pierce the mists of ignorance to find their way.

9. The schedule must go forward, it waits for no man. The entire Creation has an appointment with Destiny, that even I cannot displace. I bring MY Words of Love and pray that Man will listen. It is I who projects your life your very breath your energies, your ability to be within the dimension you find yourself. I AM with you as a part of you. I AM with you as a Creator of your very Being. I AM within you as a Father draws near to His child because of Love and Caring for that Child. I AM the Eternal Father, Everlasting Creator of all that is and Ever shall Be.

10. I am speaking to the people of the Planet as they stand on the threshold of world shaking events that will be very disastrous for them if they have not remained close to My Heart and My Love.

11. There is coming upon this planet in the very few months ahead a great need for mankind to lay aside his continual occupation with the necessities of life and take moments to yield to the necessities of His relationship with Me.

12. I will not forsake My children, neither will I suffer them to be distraught and caught in the web of dire circumstances if they will but call upon Me and give me that opportunity to be Father to them even as they are children to me. I ask only that I be permitted to show them My Love and to shelter them within the shadow of My Protective Presence and Be to them as the shade of the great oak in the heat of the noonday sun. Now is the time to become reacquainted with Me and to mend the fences, so to speak, of their separation from My Love.

13. I am He who will carry them upon My Vibration of safety and security. If they will but grant Me this request and begin to call upon My Name for their help and guidance in the days before them. I will guide them with My direction and will lead hem through the narrow pass over the rough mountains of events into a valley of peace and quietness.

14. There is no need to fear, there is no need to draw back and be consumed with human decisions, but allow Me to take the reigns of confusion in life, and lead you beyond the chaos of helplessness in events. My children walk in peaceful valleys knowing that I will always be beside them, only a thought away. Nothing shall touch them in the citadel of My Holy Mountain where I shall lead them, and they shall rise above all clamour for they are the children of the Most High. My Mighty Hosts shall gather them into the secret place and they shall abide without Fear forever.

15. In your world of sorrow and woe there is a shining glory of joy and serenity which is that place of Spirit where I dwell with all mankind. But they must seek Me and reach for My Love and be willing to be One in Heart with Me, that we might Walk Together through the gathering storm. I shall lead them like the Shepherd leads his flock into the rich pastures and places of My Presence where there shall no more be the troubled Mind. I ask this of My children that this shall be My Portion to be their Father and their God. So be It forever.

Section 4

The Descent of the Host

The Thirteenth Vortex

1. QUESTION: MUCH DISCUSSION HAS CENTERED OF LATE AROUND THE 12+1 PRIMARY SITES, CENTERS, VORTEXES. WHY 12+1, AND WHAT IS THEIR PURPOSE FOR BEING WHERE THEY ARE?

The twelve energy sites with its thirteenth compliment are in fact those primary centers in which the earth harmonic patterns are most visible and are most effective relative to the transition activities. By this we mean that there are certain points on the planet which play a major role for the transition by "anchoring" the Light as you term it. It is at those sites that those who are in harmony with the specific patterns which are projected from the higher realms will gather and make their transition. The thirteenth site is a harmonic tuning fork which will, in effect, be used to fine tune all energy patterns in the final days. It is at the thirteenth site that the beam ship "New Jerusalem" will dock and bring about that which is necessary for the completion of the planetary program now in effect.

2. These sites are most significant for those who hold the responsibility of "anchoring" the Light as they will represent the focal points for the energy patterns to be held within the earth plane.

3. QUESTION: HOW WOULD YOU DEFINE A SACRED SITE?

Sacred sites are those areas where vortexes intersect with the surface of the planet.

4. QUESTION: HOW DO WE DETERMINE WHICH ONE TO SEEK FOR?

One is drawn to certain sites because the Light patterns within their human encoding has a corresponding relationship with the ray of that Light pattern.

5. QUESTION: PLEASE DISCUSS THE "+1" IN MORE DETAIL.

The thirteenth vortex, characterized as "+1," holds a special role in Earth's transition process. It is sometimes referred to as the energy "capstone," for not only does it contain all of the encodings of the past and present planetary cycles, it also holds the activation codes that initiate the final sequence of events for the Ascension of the planet into the dimensions beyond. It is here that a "new" Light pattern is being projected that provides for all that exists within the third dimension.

6. This thirteenth ray is equivalent to a grand tuning fork that resonates the vibratory frequencies represented in the fourth dimension so that all third dimension creation can tune to the next octave of existence. Entities who visit the vortexes, will be affected by the higher frequency Light projections. If they are in harmony with the energies when they depart, they will in turn become tuning forks for others who come into their presence.

7. When Jesus Sananda walked as the Christ, this is what others felt, and healing took place directly from contact with these higher frequencies. In order to be a similar conduit for these energies, it is necessary to remain clear and balanced in all respects: physically, emotionally, mentally and spiritually.

8. High above the thirteenth vortex, know that within this area, residing in the fourth dimension, there is afloat a great vehicle of Light. Some refer to this as an energy mass, while others call it a CITY OF LIGHT.

9. QUESTION: WHY IS IT THERE?

This great ship is such a powerful energy force that it cannot enter the Earth's third dimension without adversely affecting the life streams. As such, its maximum densification is within the fourth dimension for as long as necessary to complete its purpose. Its immediate responsibility is to anchor, monitor, and adjust the incoming energies and to accommodate souls who make the transition.

10. QUESTION: YOU ARE SPEAKING OF "THE NEW JERUSALEM," ARE YOU NOT?

That is correct. It has come forth from the Moon. It has arrived in the area of Mexico and will be that which will influence the final transition of Earth into the fourth dimension.

11. QUESTION: IS THIS WHAT IS ALSO CALLED THE GREAT PEARLY WHITE CITY?

There will be many great Cities of Light coming forth into the planetary consciousness during the latter days. It is enough to know now that this great ship, which we refer to as The New Jerusalem is that which will be instrumental in the final changes.

12. QUESTION: WHY DOES IT COME TO MEXICO PER SE?

It is here that the planet is in perfect balance and therefore is able to make the transition, so to speak. At that point on the planet, there is a perfect balance between the positive and negative energy forces which makes up all that is known as Creation. Within all of Creation there are points of perfect balance whereby Creation is able to go forward beyond its existing state. When gaseous matter achieves its state from that of water, it accomplishes that at a specific boiling point whereby the balance is achieved to move beyond its current state.

13. We have difficulty bringing you information that is very multidimensional in nature. To illustrate, when you are in perfect balance with your own energies, you are able to bring forth a higher state of consciousness. Earth has an energy point within its structure, that when brought into perfect balance with its greater self has the ability to transcend its current evolutionary state.

14. Mexico represents that point whereby the harmonics necessary for this process can be put into place that will resonate throughout the rest of the planet. Mexico is the starting point of this process because of its specific origination to the GREAT CENTRAL SUN when the Earth is in its Divine position within the Galaxy. There is no other point on the planet which will be in direct alignment with the inter-dimensional pathways to the GREAT CENTRAL SUN.

15. It is the area of the Yucatan Peninsula in the heart of a triad of pyramids. The center of the Ship will be far to the north, but this is the targeting area for docking the craft. Its pointing relationship to the heavens is with your own Moon. The Moon is already in sync with the GREAT CENTRAL SUN; the Earth orientation is what we speak of here. The Earth still remains in her correct orbit to the sun, but it is within the context of the Moon that we now speak.

Sacred Yucatan
Part 14

1. QUESTION: ANY FURTHER INFORMATION ABOUT THE TREMENDOUS SHIP?

This body of energy has often also been termed a "beam ship," meaning that it is capable of "beaming" itself around while in the past stationed within the Earth's Moon. It was a vehicle of support for those who were making the rounds, so to speak, during their many life incarnations on Earth. Having departed its previous location, it is prepared now for a final docking sequence with fourth dimensional Earth in the region of Yucatan. The energy force responsible for the Earth's dimensional transition will be used for this process, plus the anchoring of the third dimensional personnel who are called to this mission. New Jerusalem will support the transition of fourth dimensional Earth into its fifth dimensional counterpart and its subsequent relocation to a multi-sun system. It is a complex energy force relationship, with all that exists within the Universe, that prevents Mother Earth from making her rapid changes and to free her from the bonds of her sun and subsequently to allow her to transport to the multi-sun system.

2. We are unable to compare this City of Light to one of your planets as requested, because it does not hold the mass, or the density, of the planets, and thus a comparison would be of little help to you. As mentioned before, it is a living organism that has the capacity to expand or contract or change form as necessary. It is a ship nonetheless, but well beyond the description outside of this linear terminology. We might add that you are going to be moving outside of this linear terminology in the near future. It is time to allow your inner feelings to take over where words leave off.

3. This glorious NEW JERUSALEM holds the magnetic properties to balance all Earth energies. It is this ship which has recently been seen of late by those who are capable of looking within the next dimension. Its size is beyond belief for those holding third dimensional perspective. Its brilliance is beyond anything known to man and its energy force exceeds that of anything within the system.

4. QUESTION: IF WE PUBLISH THIS ABOUT YUCATAN,

ISN'T THAT GOING TO BRING FLOODS OF SCARED UN-AWAKENED PERSONS AND A CROWD OF REAL ESTATE BROKERS AS IN SEDONA?

No real estate brokers are involved in this one. You can print the material received from us knowing full well that all has been taken care of.

5. QUESTION: OUR GOVERNMENT NOW HAS TECH-NOLOGY AND EQUIPMENT TO MEASURE AND IDENTIFY DIMENSIONAL ENERGIES, SUCH AS AN E.T. BEING, ETC. WOULD THEY NOT ALSO BE ABLE TO ASCERTAIN THE PRESENCE OF THIS GREAT CRAFT?

We have absolute control over all information that is received by the monitors of your government and others. They are given only that which is necessary to satisfy their curiosity, so to speak, and that which is used by our ships of Light.

6. QUESTION: DOES THIS ONE DOCKING PENETRATE ITS ENERGIES OR PURPOSE THROUGHOUT THIS HEMI-SPHERE, THE PLANET, OR ARE THERE OTHERS AS WELL AND ARE YOU PERMITTED TO DISCUSS THEIR LOCATIONS?

There will be several dockings as you have reported in *Project World Evacuation*. The significant of this great MOTHER SHIP in the Yucatan area is centered around the fact that *all other ships are a function of this one. In other words, the Yucatan docking represents the lead sequence of events for the others to follow.* There is no need to be concerned about reporting more on the other landings. These are all secondary in nature and are well known by those who are involved with them on the surface plane. The need to know about this ship of ships is what is important now, for it is a critical time to the soul awakenings of those of you who must fulfill your mission to anchor this docking.

7. QUESTION: "WE ARE THEN NOW PERMITTED TO RELEASE THIS INFORMATION CONCERNING THIS HAPPENING?

That is correct. This is an occasion that each soul most resonate to for only those who are capable of knowing will be able to do so regardless of how the information is presented in the third dimension. You are given that which is necessary for your readers to respond to within their inner Being.

8. It should be explained that all will not be ready and therefore usable to digest these things, but that the material is to be held within their inner mind for a time until their fuller awareness and all knowingness enables them to resonate properly with it. The information is sent to many for decoding their inner consciousness and assisting their awakening process. As they think on these things and take them into a process of meditation, certain realizations will be pulled through their souls toward a greater knowingness. It is enough to know that the first of the Great Cities is positioning itself for coming events and that gifted ones may indeed look upon it.

9. We do not at this time intend to get into any further revelation of the whereabouts, description or activities of the others. This is that one which is beaming forth the rays and the energies that will bring into full manifestation energies required for those who have chosen that pathway.

10. QUESTION: CAN YOU RELEASE ITS DIAMETER, ETC.?

As explained earlier, it is not a linear vessel, it is a living vessel of Light, multidimensional in its own essence, but we can say that it certainly does cover your entire area called the Gulf of Mexico.

11. QUESTION: WHO ARE ITS COMMANDING OFFICERS?

We are. The direct projections of the Eternal Throne Energies of the Universe will be recognized within the energy forces within this City of Light. The Eternal Energy forces are in direct control of all aspects of this closing sequence of planetary events. Those of the Ashtar Command are in direct contact with these who are represented within the City of Light. The way to communicate with these energies is through us.

12. *(This sacred region has been called the home of the Brotherhood, representing a vast energy network. We have been told by others it is here the order of Melchizadek has placed its seal, awaiting the awakening of human consciousness for a new beginning in the next unfoldment of Creation. The Great White Brotherhood will gather its own from many vortex areas, planted 21 million years ago within this garden, now the land of the regathering of the Lords of Light in sacred Yucatan.)*

The Solar Cross Team
Part 15

1. QUESTION: WHY DOES A VEHICLE OF SUCH POWER-FUL IMPLICATIONS AND CAPABILITIES NEED THE ASSISTANCE OF THIS EMBODIED TEAM THE FATHER HAS CHOSEN?

New Jerusalem is an energy mass that will be directly involved in the process of bringing the Earth energies in her new form through the electromagnetic null zone. It will be a most difficult task if the energy mass is not complimented by your presence, dear one, and those of your team. You will have to do your part if things are going to be ready. WE do not hold all of the strings. You are God embodied on Earth and responsible for doing God-like things to this end.

2. Go within your heart, dear one, for therein lies the Truth. Be open for change and allow yourself to be drawn without limitation to those areas to which your heart will be pulled. You have a great destiny still within the Earth plane and you must not close yourself off to the possibilities that lie in front of you. You will feel all future decisions from the heart.

3. Your balanced team, squaring the four corners of your pyramid of unit energy, as designed by the Father, is necessary because this event of docking the Great City of Light is taking place within the third dimension as a third dimension activity. Therefore the "call" must come from one in embodiment within your dimension. This pledge to the Father to undertake this Mission was a sacred trust entered into by all four of your energies before ever the breath of life was drawn for this embodiment. Identical situations occur widely in most spiritual activity that is destined to manifest upon the third dimensional level. However, in this case, because of the nature and the immensity of the project, one human instrument needed the augmentation of three more, functioning as the corners of the base of an etheric pyramid, stationed directly beneath the floating Great City of Light, to pull it down and position it into its permanent docked position for its special mission.

The Father's Energy

4. Now hear this my child. The Perfect Squaring of My Energies

61

in Mexico will be embodied and flow through this Perfect Square in these Four from My Throne. These four have united their energies again and again in many settings, in many different times, but always for My purposes and for the anchoring of My Plans and My Will upon the Earth. These two Perfect Pair are My Creation and My Planting for this moment in Time. As you stand upon the Point of Invocation at that moment in time chosen by Me, full instructions will be followed for the docking ritual.

5. *(There followed detailed and lengthy directives, instructions concerning the procedure and works to be done with the Words of Fire. Until that moment the Great Ship is afloat within the fourth dimension outside of Earth's atmosphere. When in docked mode, it will be permanently locked into the coordinates of its location within the Earth's atmosphere. All things are ready for this moment in time, awaiting only the embodied call to descend by those whose ordained work it is to accomplish this, at the Father's appointed Time.)*

6. As a fourfold compass star, these energies will be together in absolute and total harmony. In purest of love for one another from eons of time that are past. My Holy City will indeed be with men. This fourfold energy unit representative of the equal armed cross enveloped by the circle of My Divine Plan, I now call My "SOLAR CROSS TEAM" to go forth for many more assignments on a third dimensional basis, continuing your works under heaviest kinds of protection and surveillance for you are All Mine and the Angels walk with you, given charge over you to keep you in all your ways, until that time when Love and Peace shall reign on Earth as it is in Heaven. I AM THE FATHER MOTHER GOD, CREATOR. I SEND YOU FORTH IN MY NAME.

7. So be it Lord God. Holy, Holy, Holy is the Lord God of Hosts.

Section 5

Project Earth Ascension

"Love Letters From the Throne of God"

My children, I welcome this conversation with you this day. I welcome with great Love all of those who shall read My Words in this first issue of My newest effort on your behalf. I invite All to eagerly watch for My words in this space as these Letters from the Throne go forth to thrill hungry hearts.

It is not My Desire to allow the flow of anything toward any of you that would harm you. Such as may touch you or reach into your lives, your homes, will come through the Destiny of your Choices down through many lifetimes. You abide in a learning pattern. You have chosen this pattern of growth to become an Overcomer of the undertow of deafening attitudes, negativity, and ignorance. Be not separated from Me in your life.

There are great plans that I hold within My Heart for the future of this planet. It must first be cleansed and made aright, then rest for a little season. Then all of Heaven shall see what I shall do with this wonderful and beautiful abode for My Children. Ah yes, you think you know that of which I speak, but no man knows what is in store for this My Footstool, when the Great Day comes. The Earth Entity itself shall serve My Kingdom in a new way, in a new manner undreamed of as yet. We cannot release this information to your dimension at this time for many would run to and fro distorting the truth. Thus I have set a seal upon it, and closed the mouth of my messenger until you have earned the right to share in this prophesy.

But I speak in Love when I say unto you that it shall be worth all of the striving, all of the attaining, and all that you have given unto Me, when that time has come. I extend My invitation to all of

64

you to stand at My Right Hand on that day when Terra comes into
her Destiny. So shall it be. I Thy Father have spoken this Day.

The Destiny of Earth
Part 16

1. QUESTION: JUST WHAT ARE THE FINAL INGREDI-
ENTS NECESSARY FOR THE EARTH/TRANSITION/ASCEN-
SION PROCESS?

The final ingredients revolve around the desire of the "participants" to see that this transition comes to pass. It is the "participants" who hold the energy patterns that are necessary for the fourth
dimensional interface, and as such it will be upon those involved to
take control of this process through their collective effort.

2. The purpose of reflecting on Earth's future is twofold: First,
it will support one's personal awakening by triggering one's consciousness about the reason for being on Earth during these changing
times, and second, it will provide the backdrop for bringing about
"right action" relative to these end days and that which is to follow.
Many souls are programmed for specific tasks which are directed to
this "greater mission," and as such, often have difficulty in relating
to the limited teachings being brought forth about the role of
mankind in the Earth experience.

3. Third dimension Earth is soon to be transformed into a
higher frequency energy pattern. Some of the planetary consciousness is preparing to merge into the next dimension, while other
aspects will move on to other programs of existence that exist within
the vast star systems of the many and one Universe.

4. The planet has evolved through a unified effort involving
those who have been trained for this project. The time has arisen for
those souls to prepare for the final mission. There are those who will
be responsible for delivering the species from its destructive influences. This is necessary because the planet requires a cleansing which
will purge those not of the Light. Your knowledge from above has
brought a level of awareness of coming events. We now come
together with those who have been awaiting our answer to the call.
Time is now when we must act. We who deliver this message are
Light and Love and we come in the Name of God.

5. QUESTION: WHERE WILL EARTH GO IN THE SENSE

OF ITS MOVEMENT INTO THE FOURTH DIMENSION AND SUBSEQUENTLY INTO THE FIFTH?

There is a certain height of awareness needed in the planetary vibration that is required for the acceptance of this revelation. *(Note: They have suggested that after the first studying of these things, that in the sleep state which follows, while out of body, your understanding and your questions will be dealt with in higher realms of reality. Then follow with a second studying the next day, etc. until five days of rereading it and studying meditatively upon it is followed by your five nights of out of body contacts. Do it!)*

6. A "selective body" of energy composed of third dimensional Earth consciousness will enter the fourth dimension at a time designated by those participating in this program. These have demonstrated willingness to proceed along the path of original Earth mission which directly relates to the "journey beyond" and those who have made the decision and the preparation will thus do so. This does not necessarily reflect upon all those who originally encoded to do so, for much has affected the soul encodings over the course of the planetary program. Those who are ready will go as evidenced by the "self selection" process.

Transition Sequences
Part 17

1. There are several "windows of opportunity" which represent a series of sequences of circumstances on the planet, which are also related to cosmic events and energy movements that would flow through these sequences of circumstances, or Earth events. The first sequence is one in which a great deal of personal awakening is required by those who hold the keys to the particular energy pattern necessary to accomplish the transition. We must emphasize the word *desire,* for if it exists within those I speak of, there remains a possibility for this first sequence. Aside from the desire and the personal awakening there would need to be the existence of group energy which could hold the sequence, or pattern. This could be accomplished if all of those involved were resonating *consciously* with each other. Perhaps group gatherings could be used to bring together the necessary harmony among the individuals to establish the energy patterns. But each has to come into his own "knowing" for any

group to be effective. This of course becomes an essential ingredient to the personal awakening.

2. It is essential that the beings involved, who are responsible for this work, gain a mutual understanding of what is about to take place. In other words, there are those who are within the earth plane who hold specific responsibilities relative to these windows of opportunity. By gathering together, they can bring forth the forces that will support the "complete knowingness" which must be recalled if the total process is to be understood *and acted upon.*

3. You will do well to note that those events of the Sequence 1 scenario have recently been accomplished; this only recently took place. The forces in charge of this sequence of Earth events have approved the Sequence 1 scenario based on certain energy releases which took place with Earth as a direct result of such events as the China crisis and others. The energy patterns brought forth in events are related to the quality of human emotion globally quickened by those events. The inner reaction of humanity to an event, or sequence of events, affects the ability of Earth to be in proper alignment with specific energy patterns for working together as one, with her inhabitants. *(Note: There was a moment in time when the entire planet vibrated in total unity and harmony with the position taken by the heroic students in China, protested with them, suffered with them, wept with them, feeling with them on inner levels that something great had been accomplished, but not understanding its process.—T)*

4. Each who moves in harmony with his soul will be drawn to a group of "family members" who represent a great soul alignment. However, each must focus on the Christ level of consciousness before he will be completely open for merging his energies together for the benefit of the whole. When this happens, there will be a conscious recognition of what each member has to do, and what the group must do as a whole.

5. QUESTION: IS THERE A PROCEDURE IN THE EVENT NONE OF THE POSSIBLE SEQUENCES ARE SUCCESSFUL, THEN WHAT?

A "must do" condition exists in the event that the "windows of opportunity" are no longer available. All that point in space/time all systems would be turned over to the Spiritual Hierarchy in charge of this mission and an "emergency transition sequence" would be initiated. It is not one which would provide harmony for those who remain on the Earth's surface so you are not advised to look to this for results.

6. QUESTION: PLEASE EXPLAIN WHAT IS MEANT BY EMERGENCY-TRANSITION-SEQUENCE? IS IT LIKE AN EVACUATION?

It is, in fact, a form of evacuation, but like the first sequences, it would be a most difficult one, as all would most likely be in fear as a result of all the changes. We seek to have as many as possible be over any fear, and a smooth transition is therefore sought.

7. This is the last "window of opportunity" to complete the mission. We are most certain it will not be necessary. It would be a most difficult task to carry out in light of all that would be involved, for Earth is a most fragile component and she would have a most difficult labor, so to speak.

8. Regardless of which "window of events" becomes part of the plan, an Evacuation will certainly take place to assure that each is able to continue his experience according to his individual choice.

9. QUESTION: WHAT IS THE OVERALL IMPACT OF THE HUMAN DRAMA ON THIS EARTH ASCENSION PROCESS?

The human drama has been the backdrop for all the experiences sought by the soul. It has been an important facet for demonstrating the various scenarios available with the "separation" process. When it comes time to replay this scenario with a greater energy mass, perhaps the memory of those who participated in these human dramas on Earth, will be able to offer advice to others whose experiences did not incorporate the Earth plane. The human drama is going to come to an end, as you know it, for those who are ready to proceed onward. For those still seeking such drama in their lives, there will be the opportunity to cary on with such on another platform outside this space/time continuum.

Each has a soul destiny, and each at this level of experience will be able to clearly follow his original soul purpose. Some will go on board while others will journey onward to catch up later. The great "Merkabah" (New Jerusalem City) will only house specific souls who have been programmed to arrive here, after which they will go forth to their soul purpose.

10. Many energies will be transmuted permanently because they have no further function within this Universe. These are the energies that have completed their mission on the Earth plane and have no further experience to pursue. Many included in this category come to Earth to give all they had before returning to the Source of All That Is. They exist primarily as Elementals within the Earth structure which is specifically tied to a third dimensional experience. There are others who have simply gone beyond any salvageable stage and who must return to start the process all over again. These are souls who have basically cut the cord to their further evolutionary process.

11. QUESTION: WHAT ACTUALLY IS THE NATURE OF THE TRANSITION?

Transition occurs when one is capable of raising the vibratory pattern of the consciousness contained within the cellular structure of the body vehicle to a point corresponding with the fourth dimensional pattern of vibration. This can be done as quick as the desire to do so and the willingness to proceed.

12. QUESTION: IS THERE EVER A REASON *NOT* TO PROCEED WITH THE TRANSITION?

Sometimes some souls still have a desire to complete experiences within the Earth plane while others still have work to accomplish relative to the "greater" mission. You, yourself, have chosen to perform certain duties as well as many others elsewhere and will, therefore, not complete the transition process until such time as that work has been completed.

13. QUESTION: WHAT CAN BE EXPECTED TO HAPPEN TO THOSE SOULS/ENERGIES ON THIS PLANET WHO ARE NEITHER PREPARED NOR INTERESTED IN THE TRANSITION?

The majority of those of whom you speak will not be prepared for the transition, and in fact the number who will be is a quite insignificant percentage of Earth's population. Those not thus prepared will venture on to other experiences as well as continuing with those they are presently involved in. However, they shall do so on other platforms of existence. These things have been outlined quite elegantly in information given the planet about the planetary evacuation, although the term "relocation" is perhaps more easily accepted; it is, in fact, going to be the case for those who never intended to make the leap into the next octave of existence.

The Next Octave of Evolution
Part 18

1. Perceptions about what is supposed to happen in the "new age," as well as "locked in" presentations about prophesy have all added to the confusion. The intent here is not to take one out of the present moment, but rather provide some additional input for searching out the TRUTH in the eternal now.

2. The next octave of evolution is just one step up from your existence in the third dimension. It will not appear strange to you at all. Everything that you experience which is in harmony with the Light will be there. You can dream there just as you can in this dimension. This will be the source of your experience. Once you arrive in the next dimension, you will have an escort to show you around. Those who are responsible for this activity will be able to give you whatever it is that you desire in this realm. You will not have to make any special preparations other than to allow yourself to go through the doorway. Once you have mastery over this activity, you will have greater ability to work in the third dimension. You will recognize the fourth dimension by all of the beauty there. It is a place which your dreams in the physical have yet to see.

3. The Earth is going to the fourth dimension for a temporary stop which we will discuss later. The Earth can be considered just like a person. The person will continue to evolve to higher states of consciousness and so will the Earth. The Earth has desired to experience this next level of consciousness but has been held back as a result of the many forces which have sought to limit evolution. Now that she is to be freed up of those forces, she will move on. The people will move on as well.

4. Those who are in the fourth dimension have already attained this level of consciousness by experiencing and evolving through the third dimension. They will move on to higher dimensions when they are ready. This is not to say that some will not stay in this dimension to receive those who are elevated from third dimensional consciousness.

5. The fourth dimension is within the same time and space con-

70

tinuum as the third dimensional realm. This is why you can see the fourth dimension from your perspective if you have "eyes" that can see.

6. QUESTION: WOULD YOU DESCRIBE THE INDIVIDUAL'S TRANSITION TO THE NEXT DIMENSION?

You will do well to ponder on my own personal Ascension and recognize that I never really went anywhere other than the next vibratory level within the same location as I was when in the third dimensional plane. Those who have mastered the third dimensional consciousness will be able to raise the vibratory level of the physical body as I did, and then they will be raised so to speak, but within the same time/space continuum as their point of departure, once again, just moving into the next frequency of existence. It is a smooth transition for those who are prepared.

7. The fourth dimension is just a stepping stone for those who are Light Workers. For those evolving from the primary factors of life they must move through an orderly evolutionary process to be able to sustain the higher level consciousness. For those who are here to help in this process, they can return to the level from which they came with very little effort. The most difficult step is out of the third dimension, as it is the most limiting of all the realms, only because of what man has taught, however.

8. QUESTION: DID WE ALL COME FROM THE FIFTH DIMENSION?

The fifth dimension is just a passage way for all of you. When you come into your knowingness in the level of the Christ consciousness, these things will be remembered.

9. QUESTION: WHAT EARTH REQUIREMENTS ARE NECESSARY FOR THE SOUL TRANSITION?

The soul transition is dependent on the *desire* of the soul to enter into the next octave of existence and the willingness to "let go" of its current experience within the third dimension. Each soul now has available the means of moving forward with this process and as such there are no cosmic conditions restricting this movement. For the most part, in the past, there were limitations or restrictions to this process due to many factors too numerous to mention in this communication. They have all been removed and the doorways are all cleared and readied for the process to be completed by the souls who have chosen this path.

10. QUESTION: LORD JESUS, PLEASE EXPLAIN WHAT YOU MEANT WHEN YOU STATED THAT "THEY WILL ENTER THE FOURTH DIMENSIONAL LEVEL AT A TIME DESIGNATED BY THOSE PARTICIPATING"?

11. This decision has already been made by the higher self of those who represent the Earth Volunteers. You are but a fragment of this higher self, but you are a most important part, and carry with you the function of the Universe on your shoulders. Not to burden you with overwhelming thoughts, but you must come to know the greater part of the Self and have a greater understanding of how significant all of you are in these final days. WE count on all of you to pull off this mission and hope this is clearly understood. You are on Earth for this one and only purpose. The soul and its Light Body will have the opportunity to experience the MERKABAH while it prepares to journey beyond the fourth dimension. You will only remain in the fourth just long enough to prepare for that which comes next. The MERKABAH is an energy device to help the soul alignment which is a necessary process for removing any remaining disharmonies.

12. QUESTION: WHEN WILL EARTH BE REQUIRED TO TRANSCEND ITS CURRENT VIBRATORY RATE IN TERMS OF COSMIC EVENTS?

The process is primarily in the hands of those who hold responsibility for doing so. There is, however, a point in time determined by the "collective energy force" behind this mission that will require the transition to take place regardless of the desires and the then present activities of those who hold the keys.

13. QUESTION: WHAT WILL BE THE FINAL OUTCOME OF THIS TRANSITION?

As stated, the transition will take place regardless of those who may desire otherwise or regardless of whether or not the participants successfully complete their roles. However, there is an optimum set of circumstances that those who hold the responsibility within the Earth plane for this mission, should seek to bring forth. All tasks can be accomplished if all of you *maintain your focus* and remain determined. Again it is the desire which is stressed. There are no hitches other than those which are self imposed. The Cosmos has a resistance factor built in for the greater mission, but it has little to do with this "next" transition of consciousness that we now address. Take much time to assimilate this knowledge and spend more time in quiet contemplation within.

14. Once this Earth transition is completed, fourth dimension Earth will be relocated to a multi-Sun solar system. It is during this process that it will go through a transition giving birth to Nova Terra, an octave of existence that incorporates the third and fourth dimensional experiences of Earth.

15. To set the stage for "the trip beyond," it is helpful to review what is taking place during the transition of the third dimensional existence. Essentially the form or mass of Earth, represented by all of its energy components, is beginning to vibrate at a higher frequency. This is brought about by higher frequency Light projections radiating through the *primary vortexes* into that which comprise the planet. This is comparable to what takes places when an ice cube melts into water. In Earth's case, her third dimensional body is melting into the ocean of her fourth dimensional essence. When this takes place, all the experiences that were stored in the ice (Earth's consciousness) will merge into the greater body. Currently some of the Earth's life forms are resisting the melt, so to speak. By way of example, mankind has so densified its thought forms that it is not adapting to the winds of change. These thought forms must be freed-up and Earth must be fixed-up if the transition is going to be completed in an orderly manner. Compare the results of an ice cube left on the kitchen counter with one heated in a microwave oven. It is going to melt, one way or the other, but one way does a lot more shaking up than is necessary, not to mention all the extra energy that is used. It is worth noting that each soul who embodies in one of Earth's life forms, within the various kingdoms, has its own evolutionary program. Some souls will flow into the next Earth dimension while others will move onto other platforms of existence.

16. When one is part of an ice cube, a world of limitation is the natural state of being. Its slow going until the "great melt" at which point one is free to swim around in another experience. A little less density and one can float into an even freer existence. Such will be the case when fourth dimension Earth is stimulated into the next Light pattern where limitation, as we perceive it, is virtually non-existent.

The Greater Mission
Part 19

1. The planet Earth does hold a very specific purpose in the Universal Order. This has been the primary reason why the fallen ones sought to control her. Now that they have been controlled themselves in the higher realms, there is an opportunity for the planet to continue on toward her destiny.

2. Few will identify with the Great Mission. The reason that few have hitherto known the destiny of the planet is because the Father has not wished to broadcast this to all the spiritually curious for then it would only become another issue to get lost in. However, it is now time to begin bringing this to the surface of human consciousness. We will provide additional information about this purpose as time goes on.

3. It must be remembered that those who have been encoded for the Greater Mission do not represent the majority of the energy that has chosen to experience planet Earth: thus, the reason that very few will be able to identify with the Greater Mission. We therefore caution those who do have an understanding of this Greater Mission not to impose their will upon others. It would only create more misunderstanding as well as unnecessary confusion within Earth's collective consciousness. Only those who are of the highest order on the planet can be entrusted to carry forth the original blueprint of the planet. This has been presented before, only to have it fall into the wrong hands for distortion.

4. Know that the planet has been designed to bring forth the energy forces for the Throne to this sector of the Universe. It takes a very special form of Creation to handle the direct energy rays of the Father's residence. He needed to have a second Home, if you will, to further His Creation to these farther sectors which are truly a great distance from His Throne. So Earth represents a way station for the Father's energy which can then be transmitted to even farther sectors of space which hitherto have not been explored nor addressed by any of US. What planet Earth represents to the Father is the ability to further Create in an area which was unable to receive the intensity of the Father's rays which are necessary there.

5. QUESTION: IS THAT WHAT IS REFERRED TO IN THE

BOOK OF REVELATIONS CONCERNING THE NEW JERUSALEM?

That is correct. This is the specific scripture which addresses this subject, Tuella. You were guided to feature this text in your book because it is a part of the decoding that many Light Workers need in order to fulfill their mission to God. The fallen thought forms know that if this Greater Mission of Earth comes to pass, they will no longer be able to reside in the darkness that is available to them in outer space. In its Greater Mission beyond the fourth and fifth dimension, the planet will carry the Light into the far reaches of the Universe, as a free floating orbital platform which will move about according to the will of the inhabitants. Once the planet is fully prepared for her mission, she will be free from orbital concerns and will wander the universe to bring forth the Light to those areas currently in darkness.

Journey Into the Beyond
Part 20

1. Many other Galaxies and Worlds have not understood this journey of Earth into the Beyond, because they have to attain the evolutionary state represented within your consciousness. For those who KNOW, there is a high level of excitement, but to the passengers they are intense in their desire to move forward with the process. Many eyes and ears have monitored the plan for Earth as it has unfolded. Oftentimes questions remained about Earth's ability to withstand the test that she had to incur to be ready for such a journey. Now that it has withstood the test, there is a wave of excitement within the Universal Order that has yet to be experienced even when considering all that has been achieved through the eons of time and events that have resulted in the many levels of Creation as we know it.

2. The third dimension has offered a similar excitement in the past because it represented the closest experience to separation that had hitherto been available in the Universal Order. The experience of separation was not a new one, however, because in many cases it was achieved for limited states of time. What makes the Earth experience so incredible is the length of time the separation was able to be realized in the minds of all of those who partook in the Creative experi-

ence. This even includes those in the higher realms who were part of the adventure, for they, too, had to instill upon themselves the experiences of separation. *Thus the "fall" was all part of the plan!*

3. QUESTION: IN THIS JOURNEY BEYOND THE INFINITE, BEYOND ETERNITY, WILL THE TIE WITH THE FATHER/MOTHER CREATOR BE MAINTAINED OR CUT OFF? WILL HE KNOW WHAT WE PASSENGERS ARE EXPERIENCING; WILL WE FEEL HIS LOVE?

This is all very much left unknown at this point. The purpose of going forth with this plan is to see what actually will take place. You can be certain that the Father will experience a sense about what is taking place, but to what degree, at this time, is unknown. Regarding the memory, it will be erased to some extent, which is a necessary part of the process, to ensure that what is gong to take place is not altered by certain energy patterns which would resist the process. This is all very complex and a most difficult subject to phrase into words for your dimension.

Nova Terra
Part 21

1. QUESTION: WHAT IS THE SIGNIFICANCE OF THE NAME "NOVA-TERRA"?

This sacred name represents the spaceship Earth in her full glory. She will depart from this Galaxy under auspices of this Name.

2. QUESTION: DOES THE EARTHSHIP HAVE THE SAME CHARACTERISTICS AS THE GREAT CENTRAL SUN, AND IF SO HOW WILL THIS MANIFEST IN COMING DAYS?

She, Mother Earth, has been designed to function as a Great Central Sun, but she is unable to manifest such glory until all of her "crew" are on board. This is what will take place in the thousand years that follow. For her final preparations she will take on the full expression of the Great Central Sun and will be able to come forth out of the depths of her beingness. She will be in the full Glory of the Father complete with all that God brings forth from the Great Central Sun. She will be an exact duplicate of it but her dimensions will be substantially less. This is in order not to deplete too much energy from the primordial Source, the G.C.S. You must remember that we all go in the twelfth dimensional consciousness which from the

Hierarchy's point of view is the highest state of evolution achievable in this Universal Order. This is in itself a limitation of understanding which we hope to explore as well, as we journey into the beyond.

3. QUESTION: WHAT IS THE GUIDANCE SYSTEM FOR SPACESHIP NOVA TERRA?

She will be guided by the will of her people inhabitants. There is nothing more to it than that. What a journey it will be, however, for those seeking such adventure. Never before has such a guidance system been freed from all Universal constraints.

4. QUESTION: WHO IS THE FATHER TO THIS CREATION?

It is the Father Himself. He whom you know as God has embodied himself in all of His Glory into expression of this life now being given birth.

5. QUESTION: BEYOND ENLIGHTENMENT, BEYOND ETERNITY, BEYOND INFINITY...IS THIS WHAT THIS EARTH MISSION REPRESENTS TO THE ETERNALS AND GOD?

You have accentuated the mission with great clarity. Whatever is about to unfold has never been experienced before in all of known Creation.

6. QUESTION: WHAT CAN WE DO TO SUPPORT THIS PROCESS?

All is very much in order for the transition itself. Ashtar has made ready the fleets necessary for removing all of those energies which must depart Earth permanently so that this process can be completed. There is still some fine tuning to be done in order to prepare the harmonics for the final convergence. Nothing else remains other than to hold the Light and maintain the Truth of your Being.

7. QUESTION: WHO GOES ON THIS RIDE, BEYOND THE BEYOND, AFTER OUR THOUSAND YEARS WITH GOD ON THE NEW EARTH?

Only those who are ready, willing, and able to do so. Unfortunately it will be but a few of US, for those who were to be prepared at this time have chosen other paths and those paths are not going to lead them beyond. In terms of numbers, this cannot be altered, for only a few are even prepared to Ascend, which is part of their natural process. Those who will choose to go Beyond, will have a way about them which brings forth even a greater desire than the Ascension. *(Note:...Dear student, do not confuse the Ascension with the Earthship Journey, "Beyond the Beyond," as one and the same. They are two totally difference occurrences.—T)*

8. The fourth dimension, as you know it, exists for all elements that have an existence within the lower dimensions called the third. All matter is densified from a higher vibrational thought pattern, and then, in order to have a third dimension there must be a fourth and a fifth, etc. The planetary bodies seen with the third dimensional eyes do not have a fourth dimensional existence just as planet Earth. Yes, you are correct, Tuella, all within this solar system is about to make a major change whereby all frequencies are being transformed into a higher frequency pattern.

9. QUESTION: WHAT FURTHER CAN BE SAID ON THIS SUBJECT OF "GOING BEYOND...THE BEYOND?"

The "greater mission," as such, involves the processes of converting the collective consciousness *(of those who will be participating)* into a "cohesive body" of energy that is capable of responding to certain cosmic conditions permitting the transference of said energy into a dimension outside of creation itself. Not having experienced this dimension, it is not possible to elaborate upon that which is expected to be encountered nor is it possible to fully comprehend the magnitude of this experiment in linear terms. It has been discussed that the energy input of planet Earth will be able to sustain itself primarily as a result of that which has been experienced as a result of the "separation," so to speak. When the earth consciousness is combined with "greater energy forces," this "new" body of Light/energy will be able to gain the necessary momentum to project itself outside of the thus far limited nature of the cosmos. It will be at that time that the "separation" *(linear term)* of the "new body of Light" will be experienced by the Universe.

10. QUESTION: DOES THIS RELATE TO THE SUBJECT OF EARTH "GIVING BIRTH" TO A NEW ENERGY PATTERN?

When we speak of Earth giving birth to a new energy pattern, we are addressing the energy mass represented by a subset of the known consciousness of third dimension earth, which is to be merged with the fourth dimensional *(earth)* consciousness. The purpose of doing this is to sustain the memory of that which has transpired within the earth program since its inception, in order that it can be drawn upon directly by those who seek to venture beyond.

11. QUESTION: ARE YOU INDICATING THERE WILL NOT BE VERY MANY ASCENDING AT THE PRESENT STATE OF AWAKENING?

No, it is just that there are going to be many who only look at the Ascension as a process for moving into the higher states of consciousness. One has to go beyond the limits of perception in order to go beyond the limits of known experience.

12. QUESTION: HOW FAR BEHIND IS THE EARTH MISSION?

Not too much, but enough to cause great concern with those who are orchestrating the whole event. We have had to forego some of the Earth lessons which were planned, as you know, and others will be shortened in order to accommodate the greater schedule. Do not expect all of prophecy to be fulfilled no matter how convincing some may be.

13. QUESTION: WHEN EARTH LEAVES THIS ORBIT, DOES IT GO TO AN AREA WITH TWO SUNS?

That is correct, for this will be the temporary staging grounds for the preparations which must follow for the journey. She will remain in that location for one thousand years, a most busy time for all involved in the mission process. During this period, God will completely reign over this planetary body, this time when all bring forward all that is Good and Glorious. (Note: *This period is fully and completely detailed in our Holy Bible as the Heaven of the New Earth and the Presence of God dwelling with us. Further details pertaining to this period need not be referenced here.—T)* It will take approximately one thousand years, in Earth equivalent time, to complete the transition from the fourth to the fifth dimension, and to take on passengers and supplies needed for the next experience. For fifth dimensional Earth will be joined by other entities, who will be full of their own experiences, gathered from throughout the many and one Universe. Together they will become a new body of collective consciousness to be known as Nova Terra.

14. QUESTION: LORD'S...WE HAD BEST DISPENSE WITH ONE SUBJECT NOW, OR THIS OFFICE WILL BE BURIED IN MAIL. CERTAIN UNENLIGHTENED ONES WILL WANT TO KNOW THE FATE OF THE SO-CALLED KING OF DARKNESS

AND HIS "RELEASE" AT THE END OF THIS PERIOD?

The King of Darkness has not and cannot be "locked up." His thought form roams freely in the minds of those who continue to support his thought form. In the higher realms, we have long since done away with this fallen thought form and will have no need to address it again. This is another contaminated portion of the Bible which does not deserve attention. The Bible speaks of those thought forms which have yet to be reconciled in the hearts of man. When it is time, the Earth consciousness that is bound up in a semi-limited condition, will be released to proceed into the higher realms until it finally releases itself from the then known Universe. This material about the fallen ones has been distorted for so long. If souls were to contemplate this thought form, they could actually create its existence in the minds of those who will continue to reside on this planet, thus giving the dark ones a potential rebirth. The interpretation falsely existing in your Bible must NOT be permitted to deceive pure minds. Now let us move on.

15. Once Earth has merged with her fourth dimensional counterpart, she will leave her orbit around the local Sun. This process will be facilitated by the great Merkabah Vehicle stationed within the space/time continuum of Yucatan, Mexico. *The great vehicle of LIGHT is the "TUG BOAT" to MOVE THIS OCEAN OF CONSCIOUSNESS into the multi-sun star system that is in another region of the local Universe? It is there and then that all of the staging will be done necessary to travel "where no one has gone before."* When Nova Terra is in complete harmony with all aspects of its Self and tuned to the very highest known frequencies, it will begin reviving its engine, so to speak, by taking on more energy from its Source. At a point when a critical energy Force is achieved, there will be a counter balancing of the polarity that maintains Nova Terra's relationship to the Source. Eventually, Nova Terra and the Source will become balanced electromagnetically and like two magnets with the same polarity they will repel each other.

16. Electromagnetic properties associated with the Sun, along with other properties identified outside of this solar system, hold Earth into its existing pattern. Earth will come into contact with other energy patterns which will dominate existing forces. At that point in time/space relationship, Earth will release its current pattern and seek

another based on its relationship to "dominant" Forces present. It is that point which we term the electromagnetic NULL ZONE.

17. It is in this way that Nova Terra will move away from the Source, perhaps never to return again. It will, in effect, be freed from the continuous cycle of creation where everything is projected out from the Source only to have to someday return. This has been the only path of evolution because "All That Is," within the known Universe, is bound by electromagnetic properties that eventually recycle all creation through the Source. Since creation is simply vibration, its waves of energy are held in place by opposing polarities linked to the Source. Being the dominant energy force, the Source attracts back all aspects of its Self after repelling its essence outward to experience its Self.

18. In the case of Nova Terra, Source is preparing to release a part of its Self, part of its energy mass, in order to explore that which is outside of its perception of Self...no less than the equivalent of taking a look outside of creation, perhaps connecting with the source of the Source.

19. When we consciously chose to experience separation from the Source, during our sojourn on third dimension Earth, it was for the benefit of our "journey beyond." Although it has been a bumpy ride, we survived the experiment and learned what we needed to do. If time permitted, we would be able to return to full consciousness of our relationship with the Source without the assistance that we are now receiving from higher dimensional beings. Their help is needed, However, because there is a launch window that all dimensional aspects comprising Nova Terra must meet. This window coincides with the specific point when all of the known Universe begins its journey back to the Source.

20. When finished with this step, it will be positioned for yet another leap in consciousness, to what could be considered the twelfth dimensional experience. It is from this state that Nova Terra will disembark from the then known Universe to venture into the "beyond"...that is, beyond all that which is presently known.

There is Always More
Part 22

1. Beyond enlightenment, beyond eternity, beyond infinity: this indeed clarifies the Mission. Spiritual desire propels us to the un-

known for the furthering of the Creative experience.

2. Since the "beginning," Creation has continued to push outward from the Source in ever greater expansive cycles. Having once again expanded it's Self by a great thrust from the point of origination, all of what exists as Creation is preparing to journey Home: *all, that is, except...NOVA TERRA!* At the very moment when the farthest reaches of Creation quit moving away from the Source, and before reversing direction, there exists the "window of opportunity" for the trip beyond. It is at the moment of "rest" in the pendulum of evolution, when Nova Terra begins her journey into the unknown!

3. The fullness of God which is contained within this expression of life, soon to depart from its Maker, has never been explored. That, contained within this expression, is the complete knowledge of all that has been. Whatever is sought from this experience can be brought forth through that knowingness, so in other words, if it is the desire of this Creative expression to duplicate all that has come before, it certainly could do so. Contained within this expression is truly the entire known Universe which includes all of the other Universes.

4. This journey, Beyond the Beyond, is the destiny of the planet which has been our gracious host for so long. Her "Greater Mission" lies just ahead! Her name is Nova Terra. It is time to get it together if one is going to make the journey! Bon Voyage...from Tuella and Obid!

Section 6

California Coastline and the Seven Confrontations

"Love Letters From the Throne of God"

This is Jesus the Christ speaking in Love to the Family of God upon this planet.

My words come to you from the fullness of My heart as I survey the schedule that awaits mankind in this hour of its planetary history. What a grand and glorious record it has in its service to the growth of the children of God, in its provision of a platform for their evolution and growth into knowledge and wisdom of Divine Truth.

The Psalmist has said "The earth is the Lord's and the fullness thereof, the earth and they that dwell therein." *Man has been given this provision, the glorious garden on which to play out his human drama and his experiments of civilizations. He has been allotted a certain time frame in which to contain and to complete these experiments and challenges to his growth. There are spots in history that stand out as gloriously achieving all that is his finest effort, yet there remains also those dark times of his darkest search for experiencing his dominion. But now the allotted time is slowly but surely coming to an end, and the time of his accounting is before him.*

Now we must weigh all things in the balance in the accountability to the householder of the harvest. For this is indeed the harvest time when the wheat shall be separated from the chaff, and the angel who declared there shall be time no longer shall stand firm with one foot upon the land and one foot upon the sea.

Get set, my brothers, for the last moment of the great race has come. Now is the time to go for the finish. Now is the time to think of the ascension into the Great Light and prepare oneself for that moment. Much that has occupied the time and energies of even our

84

loyal Light Workers must now be laid aside, that they may attend to their personal soul's needs, their relationship with the Father, and their return to His Presence. Those who are to be sealed are sealed, those who were to be called, have been called, the time for evangelizing the sleepers, the laggards, is passed. Now it is time to prepare your own wedding garment, to see that your own "lamps are filled with oil," and to "go ye forth to meet Him. Behold the Bridegroom cometh."

The many levels of the manifest Brotherhoods of Light have blanketed your world with the messages of preparation for this planet; with calls to cleanse the human endeavor consistent with Universal Law; to align yourselves with the Divine destiny of Mother Earth.

Who will ascend with her into the next limitless level of Creation?

The Real Cleansing Mission
Part 23

1. *The removal of the fallen ones, now clustered so densely in your midst, is a basic action that clears the way for other successive measures to follow. Their presence increases the turmoil for humanity. You are Commissioned and Empowered to speak directly to these destroyers and your own voice will carry the Authority of My Decree and this shall be known by them. Know that you carry with you the full essence of the Godhead and that as you speak so shall it be. The words themselves have no special power, it is the Force and intent behind them that makes the difference.*

2. Our *Real Mission* as world serving volunteers is to prepare for the direct end time events (like Divine thermostats, not thermometers) through our *Real Power* which is projected from the Throne, for our *Real Purpose* of dispossessing, getting rid of, sending home, THE FALLEN ONES! The mission now focuses on this cleansing process, preparing Mother Earth for the Changes.

3. *It was on the third night of the ninth month of 1988 that the total Cleansing for all the upper worlds of fallen ones and their presence and influence there on all other dimensions, was totally and finally completed. The upper and lower astral and points beyond are no longer their permitted territory. ALL ARE NOW PRESENT*

UPON THE EARTH for their final days which they know to be short and fatal to their goals. In the Divine reversal of their plans, these earth-based fallen ones will represent THE MOST FORMIDABLE OBSTACLE. (Jesus)

4. QUESTION: LORD, YOU HAVE STATED THAT THESE DO HAVE A HOME PLANET IN THE UNIVERSE, A PLACE TO GO. WHY DO THEY WANT TO HANG AROUND HERE WHERE THEY ARE NOT WANTED AND CAN'T POSSIBLY WIN?

These also are the sons of God who have turned to the forbidden path. In that process as sons they were allowed by Him, to be testers, tempters of other souls in their quest back to the Kingdom of Light. Thus they, too, have had a mission, limited and circumsized by restrictions and rules. They remain because the tormenting of humans is their idea of something great to do, trying to outdo one another in this questionable activity. Many have shifted their total allegiance to the Dark Leaders. Actually some do now want to go, but are without initiative until a soul of Light requests that they do so.

5. QUESTION: PLEASE DISCUSS THEIR PLANET, CONSTELLATION, UNIVERSE ETC., SO WE CAN ASSIST.

The name of their dominion is Hades. Their planet is in another solar system. Mars has been said to be their planet, but that is incorrect. Their Universe is beyond your comprehension at this moment and unimportant. It is enough to know that they have a home to go to in other words apart from this one.

6. QUESTION: DO WE COMMAND THEM OR ASK THEM? IN SOFT TONES OR LOUD VOICE?

You are thinking in the wrong direction. It is not a matter of how you speak or what you speak. It is a matter of conviction within you that you do have this authority and you are simply stating a request that you expect to have obeyed, and of course they will know and respond. Simply tell them you speak in the Father's name, that their work is now finished and they are now to return to their home and depart from this planet, that the children of Light, and Love are now in control. They can be firmly told to lose their hold on a situation for they are trespassing on the Father's land. You will be removing those forces which have now been forced into this third dimensional realm from their exodus from above. You have the responsibility to inform these undesirables that their place on earth is no longer. This is a spiritual confrontation and not a physical one, but only those on the physical plane can continue this cleansing. You can call upon the Light, but it is you who must take the final action necessary for this event to be finalized.

7. QUESTION: WHAT IF THEY DECIDE TO RETURN?

They will not be allowed to reenter the Earth Realms for She has commanded it to be so. This directly involves your own support in that you have taken it upon yourself to set things right upon this planet. This is no time for the weak at heart. This phase of the mission takes those who are willing to accept all that comes with the job, so to speak. We caution you, this work is delicate.

8. QUESTION: WHEN DEALING WITH FALLEN ONES AT A DISTANCE, DOES ONE TALK OUT LOUD WITHOUT NECESSARILY BEING IN THE IMMEDIATE VICINITY OF THEIR ENERGY FORCE?

Tuella, you can do this, but others do not have this power. Your voice can be heard throughout the Universe, so a little earthly distance will, of course, not matter. Take note that the voice brings with it a very discordant vibration to those who reside in the darkness. This discordance is what causes them to flee, preferably to their "right place," if that is the request you bring forth. Your voice is clearly understood by the fallen ones, for they do fear you. With your request for their departure, they will be escorted by legions of angels who have assumed etheric responsibility for this effort, but you must understand that this work can only be done by another physical being.

The California Rituals
Part 24

1. I AM therefore directing the ministry of your focused energies, to cover the western coastline of this country from tip to tip, to expel in Divine ritual, the presence of the fallen ones from that important portal of Earth. *At the moment of the Call, thousands of fallen ones will gather around you and be escorted by the angels and the fleets, to their destination. The word will go forth that this opportunity will be given, and believe Me, dear one, there are many even now, who anxiously await this opportunity for a peaceful departure, knowing their time to do so has come.*

2. Please note that the Father has referred to the California coastline as an important portal of the Earth. That is because the Pacific portal is a part of the Nasca ley line, which is the most active ley line upon the planet in these end time events. His interest in that portal is also intensified by the extreme volume of calls of Light that go forth from that place from the abundance of Light Workers there. Also, of course, it is also His personal decision to prevent land inundation in that area as long as vibrational strategies concur; and thirdly, the future destiny of Mother Earth, with her all-inclusive beauty intact, is a factor. He speaks of it in this way:

3. *It is not within My Heart of My Plan that any tiniest portion of this beautiful coastline shall fall away from reality, but that it shall be preserved intact as a Great Light. Therefore, I send you to this place on this special mission, accompanied by My Great Host, dedicated to the final cleansing of Earth, who will overshadow, guide and assist this action from the skies above you, as I have requested. There will be explosions of electromagnetic help coming into you from the fleets above. As the Calls are given and as your forms travel, magnetic beams will cover that area with you. This is a journey which we will all participate in. Following the rituals in places of solitude, a response may be received concerning results or details of each occurrence.*

4. In advance briefing, I was instructed that the rituals would involve the collaboration of myself to anchor the force-field and give the Calls as the Father's representative. The fleets of the Ashtar Command overhead would be totally monitoring and controlling the removal project, in conjunction with communication and cooperative participation of Mother Earth Herself, and the subsurface kingdoms. I was still a bit dubious as to just what I was supposed to say to them, but Jesus lovingly told me:

5. *…your own words will pour forth from your heart, for this is old work for you. However, let it be remembered, we are not sentencing them to imprisonment, we are giving them personal choice to be reclaimed, and taken to their place to finish learning and growth. They are created beings also, and brothers who are simply being guided and gently reminded it is time for them to go. Give them time*

to gather, give them time to think, call in the escorts and position the angelic Hosts before you begin, then announce your Authority and state your purpose. As the trek begins, word will be passed along and thousands will gather along the course to watch but an astounding amount will participate with determination. Be aware you will be intensely surrounded with a multitude of eyes from the lower astral communities. But, Our Commands and our Legions shall be there also.

6. *The entourage that follows your journey, your rituals, is tremendous in scope. There is great rejoicing in heaven that this is being accomplished, and every word of your Calls will be answered and done. All of you will be draped with the Mantel of the masters as you stand in your sacred ritual locations, to guide these fallen ones who must now find their way back to the fold. Many will desire to be taken higher rather than to their prepared place. Many will want to accept the Father's invitation to return to His fold. This brings Him great joy.*

7. *An effusion of powerful Light will be disbursed in every direction from where the Calls originate, that will settle in over the communities to make a difference in each locale. The perfect Love that your team emanates creates a vortex that is rather uncommon and tremendously useful to the Greater Light for bringing into the third dimension powerful energies for cleansing the planet. It is not that which you do consciously, you simply serve as transformers of that Light which energizes the surrounding atmosphere.*

8. While I personally entered intensive training for this mission, I knew the Father would be selecting others to be a part of it. His directive called for two women and two males to build a balanced cross of energy. His choices were Lourdes Miranda, director of the Mexico G.A.I. headquarters and two loyal members of her staff. It was beautiful to behold the way that, one at a time, they were prepared and decoded for their mission, with soul commitments surfacing day by day. They were closely guided and assisted in a processing of the information over several months. We all received calls within our souls to blend in conscious awareness our service to the Divine Plan. We acknowledged our mission as spiritual "commandos," our Father's Cosmic Warriors if you will, aware of our own Light, aware of what was involved, committed to the Heavenly Host to work

unconditionally with them as the Solar Cross team the Father had commissioned.

9. Our Christian Era lifetimes together on the Jerusalem scene with Jesus the Christ, and Mary, and the others of which we were all aware, repeated once again, together for this crucial moment in the care of Mother Earth. The Divinely planned networking that ingeniously and inevitably brought us together, allowed us to unite in answering this call and contribute our efforts toward end times events. Lourdes was given this experience as our journey got underway:

10. I had a vision of Mother Mary and all of the Hierarchy together out in space in the Cosmos. Mary was holding my hand and she invited me to descend with her from that place, on a long, beautiful staircase. I went down and down and down with her, until finally my feet touched a podium-like place far below. There I received many flashes of past lives.

11. I looked over beyond my shoulder and saw Pepe Garcia descending another stairway and Jesus the Lord, was with him for the descent. Then I looked over to the other direction and I saw Tuella descending another of the long stairways. I saw yet another of the long stairways and Dr. Lozano was descending also. All descended to the same platform where I stood. We joined hands and proceeded to continue the descent together.

12. This beautiful vision was a source of great inspiration to all of us.

An encouraging benediction from Lord Ashtar was a joy to receive as we departed:

13. *I AM here to assure you that your journey will be totally monitored and constantly escorted and minutely participated in by the entire Ashtar Command. As you enter your areas and position yourselves for action, I will be in open channel for communication and answers from me personally. You and I have talked of this occasion many times before your present embodiment, this is like the grand culmination. Your younger brother, Pepe, is going to be totally opened clairvoyantly and clairaudiently, for this experience to be a witness and encouragement to you. I AM Ashtar in service to planet Earth and responsible for its care and protection. All of us together register our good will and Love to Tuella as she stands forth in coop-*

eration with us, and to those who stand with her in support of this work. Bon voyage to all of the Solar Cross team, we cheer you onward and go with you every step of the way. We are the Winged Brotherhood of Light At Your Service.

14. The Lords of Light also gave a benediction of comfort:

The dark ones know that this activity concerns them, regardless of their attitude. They will not attempt nor interfere or bring any harm or danger to any of your persons for there is already that agreement in place, with the Lords of Michael's Bands. A certain agreement has been made for this safe passage for those who desire to go.

15. I was instructed for the journey, to consciously build an impenetrable wall of White Light every mile of the way as we travelled, like a bulldozer pushing over the terrain. The ships of the fleets were to expand that Force-field of Light 100 miles to the east, 100 miles to the west into the water, 100 miles to the north and 100 miles to the south. The designated locations for rituals were approximately 100 miles apart, but not always exactly, but the Light emanations overlapped on them all. I was specifically told to always address the Higher Ones first before speaking to the fallen ones. Lord Jesus said that these would all destroy everything the Forces of Light were trying to, and that was why there cannot be any "trespassers" remaining on this planet. *"It has been willed and given to those of God's finest, Highest Order, and they shall inherit the cleansed, perfect, New Earth."*

16. A very forceful and instructive message was given concerning the dark ones on this day:

We in the higher realms are beginning to see the effects of the Light penetration thus far that has currently been activated on the planet. It has a profound effect upon those of the Light, and as expected it has stepped up the dark forces in their effort to maintain their control. They know that time draws near for their removal, and they will continue to disrupt the efforts of the Light Workers as much as possible.

17. *The best defense is to always stay in the Light and when confronted with a dark energy, proceed with calling in the Forces of LIGHT. We will then be able to take over using the higher energy forces available to us. We are encouraged by those who are able to*

discern and welcome the opportunity to support the cleansing from above. We can only come when called, as this is the way of the Father. It is the call that is made from third dimensional realm that allows us to enter into the affairs of that dimension to resolve that which is out of harmony. We are able to do this whenever a call is made.

18. Lord Michael's warning is shared for your enlightenment:

You will call to these forces of darkness and make it known to them that their right place is not of this planet. Call forth the Light to shine brightly upon this truth. I, Michael, will be with you to call out My Legions of Light to demonstrate to those who are of the darkness, the powers which have been entrusted to you. Call upon Me to make this known whenever you see the need. Never hold back. I will come in the full force of the Godhead.

19. *You will be up against the masters of deception. They will attempt to trick you and will only have success if you try to do this on your own. You must not try to meet these fallen ones head on without your calls being made to us. This can be very devastating to you and the mission. If you were taken out of embodiment before your time, you would have to reenter through a walk-in process and there is little time for this. This issue of time is so very critical that even you do not have the complete comprehension of that which is involved here. We cannot make it any more clear to those of the Light about this critically short period of time which we have to clear this lower realm and to make way for the changes for Mother Earth. We must all now pull together. Do you clearly understand that We* **must become a conscious part of this process.** *You have done battle with the fallen ones before, so none of this is new. The only thing that is new is the* **level of deception** *that resides in those who have now taken refuge on the physical plane. They are very powerful beings who can only be contended with through the Forces of Almighty Lord Michael. I am certain that you now understand what I am saying, so now let us move on.*

#1 Bodega Bay
Part 25

1. The Father had previously said: "*It may always be assumed that all events occur on three levels simultaneously: physically, men-*

tally, and spiritually." That observation apparently also applied in my later instructions to share all details of the experiences with the family of THE THRONE CONNECTION. Plainly it was my work to activate from the third dimension the rituals and calls that would precipitate the ordained results. This to be assisted by the energies of the rest of the team. It soon became apparent that Pepe's work was to be the eyes of the team, reporting clairvoyant what was to be seen around us, above us and so on. Back home, my daughters Eve Goldman and Donna, synchronized their meditation with the rituals, working from a map, as instructed by Ashtar, to record the etheric results of each ritual. (On Cosmic levels, daughter Eve is known as ELLYSSA. Henceforth in these reports, she will be referred to by her Higher Self name.)

2. With the long trip from Salt Lake City behind us, we eagerly arrived at Santa Rosa. Sonoma County is truly a place of beauty which made the trip pleasant across the inland span to Bodega Bay and the seashore. The Solar Cross team approached Bodega Bay Sunday evening at twilight time. The bay was comforting in its quietness, with only the sound of a lonely fog horn far away. We gathered our blankets and chairs to sit at the windy waters edge amongst the growth in the sand, quieting ourselves immediately to create our Force-field. We individually expressed thanks and dedication and called upon the Father to assist us in constructing this Force-field for the mission. We spoke to Mother Earth to express our love for her; announced to her our presence and that we had come to help her, and blended our voices in the use of the nine sacred Om's. We received confirmation from the Angelic Host that they were all in position and the Ashtar Command was now thick over our heads. The time spent on the Force-field itself was very important. It was uplifting to monitor its size and power and the manner that it seemed to increase with each use. It was totally impenetrable by those opposing the mission. With the vortex created and expanded, there at the waters edge we began our contact with the fallen ones, speaking to a vast crowd of them in great detail. We spoke in the vibration of Love, carefully explaining the Father's plan and will for them. It was made absolutely clear their work here was finished, that they must now leave with the angels who were here to help them, and closed with the fiat for their departure from Earth. We left the results

in the hands of Lord Ashtar and the great fleet, Lord Michael and his Legions of Blue Angels, Beloved Mary, and Jesus the Christ and all of the Hierarchy to complete what must be done. We remained silent within our Force-field for perhaps ten minutes or more after which we shared our insight and impressions. (These details will not be repeated, since the rituals proceeded in much the same pattern.)

3. We were totally united in the witness that many were being swept upward and escorted by the angels and were being received into the waiting ships. They were significantly most willingly entering into this departure, as if the decision had long been thought out and carefully made. I sensed much relief in their midst that their deliverance was at hand.

4. Pepe gave us this visual report, transcribed there and later translated: August 20, '89, Bodega Bay, CA.

When we first arrived at the Bay, I saw a powerful Light and many great Ones with us. I saw Mary, Jesus, and Lord Michael standing together and many angels above us and around us waiting for the call to begin. I also saw the others, gray silhouetted, some without physical form, some only in shadows, and a throng of them from far out into the sea. Hundreds after hundreds of them, without defined shape or faces. There were also many hundreds of them coming out of the soil, behind and around us. When the special fiat was given for them to depart to their special place, I watched them being drawn to the brilliant column of Light coming from beneath the ship and then raised into the ship. The atmosphere was very calm and quiet. All was in order and no confusion. The ritual had been very powerful. I was given the perception that around ten thousand or more than that, but near that number, had been removed from that place through the ritual.

5. Before that, as I looked on the bottom of the ship, I saw the bay doors where scout ships launched and returned. I saw that these doors, when closed, had the Solar Cross Insignia, but when they opened, the four parts of the Cross became opened outward. After the doors were opened, then the brilliant beam came through that opening also. As I was amazed at the column of Light, I was told by them that the circumference of it would be related to our team unification and harmony, that the power of our unit Force-field would determine the diameter of the beam. That was a special message

from them. They further said, *"Now is the time to begin the work within yourselves, to do that work upon yourselves, that only you can do. They told us that each day was a further working within us preparing us personally for the work ahead in Yucatan which would be a more difficult mission."*

6. I also perceived how after our Force-field had been built, its shape was lake a Solar Cross that extended into the depth of the whole planet, sustained by our own solar cross energy field.

7. Later, I was deeply moved by the overshadowing of Ashtar as I received his first channeled message:

Good evening, my beloved friends. I am Ashtar, leader of the fleets for Our Radiant One. This evening, I come to bring words for this special earth-based unit. This is my first time to speak with you Pepe. Do not hesitate to write, just let my words flow from within you.

8. *The first cleansing work that Tuella has just finished was a complete success. A tremendous mass of beings were removed from this area of earth, numbering about ten thousand. When the cleansing action was completed, a luminous trail of Light remained over the entire area visible for a great distance beyond here. All of the scheduled cleansings that are planned will provide maximum Light energy to all of the western coast assuring that when transition changes come, they will occur in a smoother, gentler manner.*

9. *The power of all of your combined energies generate such strength that any location which you touch remains magnetized with your Force-field and this has been seen in all of your travels as we have accompanied you. Remain calm and confident, working and providing your energies in the service of Our Radiant One. I say goodbye and close my message. I Am ASHTAR.*

10. At home, ELLYSSA recorded this vision, later transcribed for this report. Ritual #1, Aug. 20, '89, Bodega Bay.

"I visualized the four of them at the Bay and immediately I saw them as four corners like a pyramid base. A golden cord of some type is being pulled from within them. It is an energy, it becomes four sides of a pyramid which I feel being lifted higher and broadly spread outward. There is a second pyramid beneath the upper one, possibly a reflection, but they are base to base and the second one is pointing downward into the soil. The pyramids begin to rotate together, spinning faster and faster, creating a form of chain link circle around the base lines of the double pyramid. Like a tornado action, the more it spins, the more it begins to pull into it at the bottom, and the more it spins forth stuff out of the top. It's pulling up *stuck energy!* I sense it coming out of the toxins in the water as well as the acid rain accumulated in the soil. Just a heaviness, literally being pulled up out of hot air, the water and the land, and consequently even out of people in that large area. If the Solar Cross team can just remain there for at least an hour the circumference will expand and reach down to San Francisco and north to Eureka.

11. As I watched it, I could see that it looked like a putrid pus, odorous pus like a gangrene infection would have. It is continually being pulled out, but I notice that if you could remove the greyish white element of it, the green and yellow remain. Now the offensive odor is letting up and its beginning to smell like a clear, breezy summer day. I'm feeling that the people of this entire area will gain a lot of mental clarity, that clouds of confusion and karma have been lifted from them. There has been such a mass happening of murders in that area the last six months. People destroying their whole families, or drowning their children, really heavy stuff and they do not know why they are doing it. I feel that kind of thing removed, lifted off.

12. The drought of their land is letting up; we'll see less forest fires there. The green will bring the balance in. The rain will be as it should be and the earth will have a kind of rest there because of this ritual. I see the area colors of green and yellow clearly. The yellow is spread across the ocean shore, the green spreads out over the vast area. I see that two very prominent Beings are going to locate there, if not already, to anchor the green and yellow rays. Entities with huge amounts of yellow within their being, who have lifted their intellects to tremendous heights of wisdom. The green will be someone in the medical or psychological fields, with also new ways to grow food for health, someone with a huge green aura, clear and bright. Not that they necessarily do these things, it's who they are, and that they are there, that matters. Movements come out of these two colors resulting from this ritual at Bodega Bay. This particular area has the greatest number of AIDS victims, and I feel these two colors bringing in a balance to that situation. I am also sensing that these two individuals mentioned to be women, embodying the nurturing needed to be anchored there.

13. Further, I see that Mother (Tuella) and her solar cross team, the four individuals, as corners of the pyramid, have come from a lifetime as two sets of Kings and Queens from an area directly through the globe to the opposite side which was once land. These four cooperated in this same way 26,000 years ago at the closing of another cycle. They also will benefit from the clarity of the green and yellow that I see pulling through this geometrical shape. They benefit personally and karmically from it.

14. It is difficult to describe what they are now showing me, as I attune to the ritual. I see many huge angelic beings. I do not distinguish appendages, just hugeness, bigness, tallness, and they are together pushing the energies out to the perimeter of the area. They are tuning into all calls that have been made from there by those who Love God, whatever their theological or philosophical positions might be, calls of all of those who have called to heaven for help. These Tremendous Ones, have gathered up all of these calls and they are pushing them through what appears to be like a big green garden hose. They are using the combined energy of the calls to scoop up more negativity into the suction of pyramids so that the circle perimeters are affected. Rape and murder statistics will drop in the area.

15. Now they are showing me a beautiful apple tree. It is huge and healthy and filled with golden apples. Vitality, health and abundance. Someone is DEFINITELY going to move to this coastline area who will feed the people their wisdom. It's as if that symbolic, smelly pus had been allowed to remain, these teachers couldn't have come. The great apple tree is a perfect circle in shape, to fill the geometric energy pattern over the area. After this ritual, two new movements will come down here and create lots of change. All of the people in that 200 mile radius, who have pure cool green and clear yellow in their auras, will find their careers beginning to fly. Those with these two colors perverted to dirty green, dirtied yellow, etc., will suddenly find blocks to their work. Only 49% of the pure color remains, winding down their careers and influence.

I see many people leaving that area now, because of family breakdowns, financial breakdowns, career breakdowns, writers block, etc. But many others will experience the attraction to clarity there. I recall that many new hospitals are being built in that area.

(As the girls completed recording their meditation of this ritual, Commander Ashtar joined them with a beautiful statement of thanks and appreciation for their assistance and participation in this tremendous project to be reported to the people, who also have participated.)

#2 Carmel-By-The-Sea
Part 26

1. On the second evening, we were led to the water's edge in the center area of Carmel-By-The-Sea, below Monterey peninsula, a very quaint and beautiful town which I loved on sight. It had a wonderful vibration, and it was there we gave out Calls, our thanks to the Father, our devotion to Mother Mary, proceeding with the force-field work and then the exhortation with the fallen ones.

2. This time we noticed and discussed together the willingness of the fallen ones to enter into this departure, not only peacefully but with a seeming enthusiasm for the exodus. The first ritual there showed a marked measure of hesitancy, a certain coyness of manner but an obvious desire for participation. This night that was changed. They literally poured into our area and into the beam with gusto. On the first encounter, I realized we were surrounded by a wall of many faces and curious eyes, yet with comforting knowledge that we were within the care of the Angelic Host and the Ashtar Command and that we would simply proceed with that which we had come to do. I allowed love to flow through my being as I spoke with them. But, during this second ritual, I was aware that the crowd behind us was of so much lighter a vibration. I had commented upon the presence of four beings standing to the side of us. I didn't want to turn and look directly, because I didn't want them to go away. Then, gradually, a great crowd manifested behind us, over toward the houses and the built up area. I asked my team if any of them saw these things or could confirm them and they answered that they did.

3. For me, the highlight of the evening was the presence of three UFOs just to the left of us, looking somewhat starlike until the largest one began to move. We watched with pulsating hearts as it swung to and fro, and slowly went up and down, and moved a great distance to the north. Then we noticed another nearby "star" that began to move, and I observed to the team that, "They usually come in three's." Then we all spotted the third one. We were graciously treated to a wonderful exhibition and communication, remaining for a considerable time, thrilled to know that they were there, and that we were all aware of each other.

They informed us that their purpose was to monitor the result of the cleansing. Because of this, they were unusually low on the western horizon. The sun had set. We had been allowed to enjoy its beautiful colors as we began our vigil by the sea. We remained on the spot until they all moved on northward for their work along the western horizon of the coastline. It was indeed a wonderful evening.

AND NOW WE SHARE WITH YOU PEPE'S REPORT:

4. When we arrived at the ritual place, I immediately saw a huge star-like ship. Following the building of the force-field and the invocation, I saw a glowing pink light ascending from each of our hearts and directed to the center of our hands, creating a pillar of Light that extended outward and upward everywhere, through all of the cardinal points surrounding the entire planet. As I watched the Ashtar Command overhead, directly above us, I focused on a ship which had a solar cross opened like four bay doors outward, expos-ing its brilliant white light beam. The crowd of fallen ones began to dislodge the area and approach the great light beam with the angels helping them. I was amazed to see a dark appearing ship arise from the ocean water and swiftly head into the beam.

5. Across the bay, I saw another, larger starship similar to the one above us. Four smaller ships were positioned around it helping it to remove those who wanted to leave. They also had the Light beam projecting downward from the craft.

6. When all of the work was finished, my attention was drawn to a smaller ship just a few miles to the left of us and low on the edge of the sea. I became aware that it was monitoring the level of the vibrational frequency, checking the entire area for many miles, wait-ing for anything further to surface, and registering all of the infor-mation of the whole occasion in their records. Two of the ships were doing this, monitoring all of the changes in the energies of the broad area where we were.

7. Then three of the craft joined together at the close of the

evening to produce for us a real manifestation of their presence. We saw a great show put on by them, they seemed to be so loving, answering my questions and doing clever things with their craft. Their movements were gradual, gentle at first, then rocking to and fro and many things. We were speechless as we remained in fixed attention upon their loving performance and delightful exchange. They reported on the new clean vibration that filled and penetrated the area, and that they would continue monitoring the area in that way. We were comforted in the thought of the nearness and cooperation of our Friends just over there across the water and an evening's work well done."

• • •

At home, ELLYSSA recorded this vision:

Ritual #2, August 21, 1989, Monterey/Carmel coastline.

8. ELLYSSA: "As I see them again, forming the pyramid base, this time it is anchored on the ground, and I see a blue flame from it. It is more like steam from within the pyramid that is coming out at the point above. Instead of a suction inward this time, there is a floating outward of something like purified particles of air. There is, this time, much more force with it, in that the pyramid is solid on the ground, with this blue sword kind of energy around it, to slash through something that is affecting the spiritual and political leaders as well as some strong thought forms that prevail which require powerful cutting through to loosen them. I am feeling that this ritual is gong to be more active in freeing up trapped Light Ones, than ridding us of the dark ones. I am being shown a scene from the fairy tale, where the Prince had to slash and cut his way through dense undergrowth to reach Sleeping Beauty. This blue that is released in the Carmel area now, is sent to cut through and reach a large body of Light Workers, church workers, politicians, whatever, that are trapped within a maze of old thought forms, old patterns, old mental baggage."

9. There isn't anyone behind or holding the swords. I just see them floating around above the area, slashing away in all directions. The swirling within the pyramid causes these swords to fly like arrows so that there is no warning. I am not seeing any Beings wielding the swords, and the thorns are not resisting the onslaught. The

silver blue swords are whirling in great speed and the thorns don't know what hit them. The thorny mass almost looks like rolls of barbed wire rolled with undergrowth entwining. The people on the other side of it are literally trapped in the sense that they can't get through it to do what they are supposed to be doing.

10. Where yesterday's energies were expanded outward broadly, this blue energy is reaching upward and higher. The energy is being swept through the astral and etheric level, because there are souls waiting to incarnate to become strong spiritual and social leaders, but have been unable to do so because of this tangled mess surrounding this space. I have a sense of a lot of it being a martyred sense of consciousness of many of the Light workers. I see this being sliced out so that carnate individuals can complete their work and incarnate volunteers can come. Yesterday's energies were very definitely physical, with the water, the ground, the vegetation and so forth but with today's energies, only about a third of it is with living people. It is the astral and the etheric of this space that is even more so being touched by this ritual.

11. This Carmel-Monterey area has good positive blue energy anchored; in other words, they are being responsible, they are willing to take authority. They are going to experience an increase in their various memberships. But those who do not have this blue energy, those who maintain, "This is our little belief and no one can change it...etc.," who feel no obligation to what is going on in the world around them, will experience a diminishing of their constituency. Politically likewise, there will be a shifting in the voting pattern as the willingness to take responsibility becomes contagious from the leaders to the followers. Until today there has been a kind of trapped leadership in those areas.

12. There will also be an improvement in the quality of the very air, because of those old thought forms that are being cut out, slashed away. Taking deeper breaths of responsibility and awareness. The work seems to be more with sleeping volunteers than with the sluggish ones who get in the way of the others, who become so accustomed to running into resistance that they just give up. Now with the coming of these swords, I see some of them sitting up, standing up, looking around a little, and realizing their first job is to sweep out the debris from the action of the swords. 'Let's break these

ideas down and just see how harmful they really are.' I have also seen the thorns as representing bickering between the systems, so I see this energy bringing in more cohesiveness and a working together. I see this ritual of Tuella and her team on this day accomplishing great and long term improvements for this Carmel area.

13. Also in this area they are going to see an increase in the birth of baby boys. Young Knights, who have not incarnated in a long time, male souls who will lift the vibrations of manhood. Not the rebellious type of souls, but those willing to take on heavy responsibility. I see 200 to even 300 of these coming who had been trapped in the astral unable to make it through.

14. Whereas yesterday we saw the Angels who spread the effects circumvently, in this energy it is the people who do it. For instance, realizing a certain thing has worked in one area they volunteer to go to another area and try it. A people generated expansion of blue flame determination on the move. Once the swords had shot through and cut something, the swords fall to the ground, but then I saw the people picking them up and continuing to use them. They were ready to own up to their power, and I saw that the blue flame coming out of their mouths was TRUTH. And I do see a crusading action of these people overlapping the ritual area into the neighboring circles, even the green and yellow of yesterday.

15. People on this level, carrying the sword work, yes, but I also see that on the higher levels, I see astral and angels and etheric beings, picking up the swords that have been hurled higher, and continuing to use them, so that the perimeter is being heightened as well as expanded.

• • •

16. DONNA, present with Ellyssa, was also permitted to see the pyramid and the swirling action within it, and the blowing out everywhere of the swords. She recorded:

I saw the sweeping up, the cleaning up after the cutting, slashing work of the swords. It reminded me of the clean up crews following a hurricane. I didn't see any angels either. It was the people I saw who were cleaning up the clutter and lifting up the swords. I noticed the swords were different shades of blue. Some were very shiny, some were oily and dusty looking, some were very delicate light blue, others brilliant blue, but all were blue. I knew that the angels realized they could stand back knowing these Light Beings incarnate would do the job and carry it on. The people had to do their own cleaning up, it was as if there was something they had to recognize, something they had to work on, knowing it was THEIR STUFF so to speak. As the cleansing pushed into the higher areas, I saw the same things take place on those levels.

17. ELLYSSA added these words: "Where yesterday Kuthumi and Hilarion seemed so involved, today this is definitely Lord Michael's energies controlling this ritual at Carmel-By-The-Sea."

#3 Santa Maria
Part 27

1. The third ritual was destined to be a different one from the start. On the evening before, attempts of a unity destroying nature surfaced and threatened our team peace and harmony. It was a totally sleepless night for me as concern for my beloved team crept over my soul like a fog. A string of insights and revelations poured into my consciousness, exposing the means, the tactics, and purpose of the opposition. Clear guidance followed on that which must be done. I had to activate the blue flame to prepare for the coming ritual at dawn. In spite of no rest, I felt a surge of inner power at daylight. (However, later, I spent most of the day asleep en route.) It is comforting to know that every attempt by the dark ones to separate us from the Father's Love and Will, only works to strengthen that closeness with Him, and each other. Thus Love prevailed all the more.

2. At sunrise, west of Santa Maria, on August 23rd at the Guadalupe Lake coastline, we positioned ourselves to begin the ritual. I immediately became aware of the piercing attention of a powerful Prince of the Underworld of fallen ones, who had come to observe and certainly not to leave! I did not fear him, but neither did I underestimate his strength. I didn't particularly desire him to be a part of the ritual audience.

3. Pepe gives us a good and totally correct report of the moment, transcribed at the scene and translated from the Spanish by Dr. Lozano, who did all my necessary translations. Pepe speaks:

4. When we arrived at the Guadalupe Lake area, a strong energy seemed to make things difficult for me because I felt a prob-

lem of heavy darkness surrounding us. We began to build and generate the force-field and completed it. I felt a sphere of Light around us, above us, beneath us, and surrounding us. It was about 200 miles in diameter. But I saw that the rays from our force-field were broken by the negative ions and that outside of our sphere it was very black. We were in the very core of it, like the eye of a hurricane. There were packs of fallen ones surrounding us and I could perceive they were the tallest ones I had ever seen. I sensed them as being followers of the Dark Prince that Tuella had seen and told us about. As this legion of dark ones had come in they brought with them an elongated very dark cloud that covered the entire western horizon north to south. As a matter of fact, it was in the news that next day that somewhere just north of us, there had been snow on this morning of August 23rd!

5. Tuella called in Lord Michael and the Ashtar Command to deal directly with the Leader. I saw that when we invoked the Lord's Hosts and the Command, the dark crowd withdrew quickly a great distance back. After the invocation, I witnessed many Light rays piercing the area so the space craft could enter it. Those who volunteered for removal were taken into the ships; however, I sensed that the giants I had seen before were refusing to go, so they were courteously ignored. I was told that this multitude of fallen ones removed this morning was the greatest removal of all of the rituals thus far. It was exceptional, in that it also included throngs of them coming out of the sea, enormous crowds of them. There were also multitudes who came from across the land and a larger number of ships were required but they were ready.

6. I am so glad we have Pepe's reports for all of you to enjoy. In spite of this manifestation from the opposition, there were more departures of those who dared to resolve to leave, that morning, than at either of the other two confrontations. Forty thousand had been reported as the harvest at Carmel, and this day there were more than that who greatly wanted to go.

7. The long black cloud was slowly but surely approaching us as well as sharp, cold winds. We hurried backward away from the water, and the storm approaching across the waters. We dared not linger, feeling very uncomfortable there, and left hurriedly to go for some breakfast, but even before being served, I shamelessly fell

asleep at the table. Later, we continued on, stoping in the afternoon at one of the old missions at Santa Monica. There Lourdes received a message from Mother Mary. She informed us that those who had opposed us this morning were Principals and High Leaders of the Dark Kingdom, and that they and their immediate followers had no intention of leaving the planet voluntarily, now or any other time. As Mary spoke with Lourdes in the old mission chapel, she also mentioned that she had been standing with us that morning by the sea.

8. Exhaustion was beginning to surface within the team. We had reached a state of numbness that swallowed up the demanding grind, while nights of healing and restoration knit the reveled edge of our beings. This was all important, for all of us were very aware that our physical temples were being used as transmitters of Throne Energies as we moved along the highway. We had agreed to this.

9. That morning, our mediators at home received the following information. ELLYSSA speaks into the recorder:

"This time I see Lourdes alone, with the other three around her with their hands out feeding energy to her. At first, I thought she was standing still, but then I realized that she is moving very slowly clockwise, and I feel a very deep purple around her, forming like a column, something like a high dunce-type cap. A real thin circular pointed thing, not big like a mountain. Its real small and rises above almost like a monolith. I see the others feeding energy into her. I feel she was chosen for this because she had the most purple in her aura. After impact of the purple energy, it thins and rises taller and taller. This column of this particular energy is rising higher than any of the others, even beyond etheric, up to the celestial and Throne levels, where all ideation begins, intelligence without form. She is piercing at the highest thinnest point so that a conduit is being formed between the bottom of the cone to the very top, going into this pure intelligence layer, so that old ideas which hide mysteries, such as secret orders, or individual special messages...that all of this information locked in the pyramids and that kind of thing, will be displaced with a clarity, an acceptance and an understanding of formerly so-called mysteries. What this ritual had done is to create a conduit, or funnel, to bring the many mysteries of truth down into this three-dimensional layer, information that is hidden, so to speak, whether in books, places or whatever. It is breaking up some kind of seal upon Truth, in a series of seals, and with this one definitely being a purple one."

10. "In the first two rituals, you were swept up in the velocity, the speed of the action taking place, but this purple energy feels very, very slow. Very deliberate, a sense of having to be really looking closely to see any movement. Therefore, the breakthroughs in this area are definite but not as quickly visible as the first two. Because of what the Solar Team is doing with this purple coned energy in that area of Santa Maria circle, they have created an opening for an individual who will become attracted to this area; who is one who seems to have the key to many mysteries; whose past life memories are very clear and will know how to properly interpret. A most unusual type of person, to continue to anchor the movement that this ritual has started. The people's 'need to know,' may lead to the creation of a newspaper type release that will feed people this kind of information. This cleansing action is that which will remove the foolishness and fads, nd false entertainment, and all the gimmicks of the New Age Movement. That people will begin to want to go straight to the Source Within because of the focus of this purple cone energy. There will be fewer psychics attracting people through phenomena while the deeper and more spiritually Wise Ones will be awakening others to their own God Self and inner information."

11. I also saw that this purple cone energy would strongly affect the four doing the ritual, in the sense that if there is anyone on the planet who owes any of you a personal debt of a good deed, money, energy, or anything due to you, that this cone will remove any blocks that keep good from coming to you. Not necessarily in a monetary way, although I saw that happening on the first day, but more on a psychological, emotional kind of support, validation, an increased awareness that people know you are here, and a deeper level of attentive listening to what you have to say.

12. Also the fact that the cone is so very, very high and pointed indicates that people are hungering for clear-cut, pointed answers having grown weary with garbled, wordy, ministrations. There is definitely an individual coming in to that area around whom a new movement will cluster which will dispense a clearer kind of information that will remove confusion. Purple is also a color of maturity. Many are lingering in the indigo uppers of the blue, but the release of

this purple cone energy will lift them up onto their next level of expression spiritually. In the rainbow, even though the purple is the narrowest of the colors, it is located at the bottom, there sustaining the weight of the entire rainbow in terms of color. It is as if the purple individuals carry the weight of mankind on their shoulders. This ritual has expanded to touch everyone on the planet to awaken them to their kharma: their agreed responsibilities for the human species. I definitely had this sense with Tuella and Lourdes and the other two, that this is their lifetime of making a contribution, and making a difference to awaken other sleeping teachers of teachers. Too many sheep are going astray because they have no teachers, as the teachers of the teachers need awakening.

13. I noticed that the cone becomes so narrow and so sharp that it becomes like a needle…because of this purple cone energy released in that area, people will read things with an immediate sense of knowing it is or is not the truth. A strong "knowingness" will prevail. Old lifetime memories will be stirred. Purple is definitely a maturing color and it will pull people out of the things they tend to get lost in. And I sense that because of this ritual and the release of the purple energy, a very High Avatar will be able to turn up his clock as it were, and be able to appear much sooner than otherwise …because one of the parents who had agreed to parent him is more aligned now to do this. An Avatar will come in on the purple ray now, because of this ritual, with the power and the majesty of it, and the willingness to be a Leader of the species into what is next for the planet.

#4 Santa Monica
Part 28

1. The Santa Monica area was the site for the fourth ritual. As we sat at the water's edge to begin, we felt the eager ones first standing quietly at a distance away of about 100 feet, then finally pressing closer to be taken by the Angels and the Commands. Again a large starlike craft was above us. It did not move erratically, only in a slow, gentle movement. The date was August 24th. Pepe reports:

2. I received a message from the ship that their presence was with us to be a part of our protection and for monitoring the ritual procedure and the results. Other ships handled the departures.

As Tuella was giving the Call, our force-field proved to be extremely large, appearing as concentric circles upon water. The energy field continued to expand and expand to a tremendous coverage, many miles in diameter. At the seashore very near to us, I saw an incredible spaceship, the size of a stadium, with many smaller ones surrounding it.

3. As the ritual proceeded, I could see how the masses of fallen ones were drawing closer to all of the ships with the Angels assisting them to do so. I sensed their extreme willingness to do this and their being very disposed to the departure, going quietly and with no resistance. There were no resistors present. After the cleansing was all completed, we felt a much lighter vibration everywhere in that special place in comparison with that which prevailed when we arrived.

4. I marvelled within myself that anything so eventful as the activity we were engaged in, could nevertheless become almost routine. This ritual was routine only in the sense that everything went smoothly and well. Our coordination with the heavenly team above us was working like a well-oiled machine. But the metaphor, or vision, that was given to our "Watchers at Home" was to me a tremendously exciting report.

ELLYSSA recorded these words:

5. My immediate sense of this ritual reminds me of the great Sun God plaque. The ritual is symbolized by a huge Gold Circle. I saw all four of you in a circle, but with your backs to the inside of the circle looking outward, holding hands. I was given thoughts of the Gods of India, how some have the eight arms. Somehow I FELT A VERY STRONG POWER in all of your arms, and that in the connecting of it, in the left knowing the right of the person next to him, encasing this circular space for this gold to show up. This huge Golden Circle is not moving clockwise or counter-clockwise, but is rather beginning to form from within its outer boundary, concentric circles within it, evenly spaced, into the center tiny one. For example, if a circle would be within you, then the next one would be just barely outside of you, and then they would just continue to expand in these concentric circles. I saw that there were eight circles, and that each one was twice the distance of the one before it. Were I to draw it, circle two would be one inch from center, circle three would

be two inches outward, circle four would be four inches outward and so on, because the energy keeps enlarging and pressing outward.

6. Realizing that Gold is precipitated sunlight, and knowing that gold symbolizes the intellect and the male Godhead, The Father, and understanding that the area needed the gold, I was picking up definite mental distortions in the human pictures people hold about God. Connecting more to the Power that is God, rather than the concept that He is a long bearded entity just keeping a record of whether we're naughty or nice or whatever, but realizing the Creator as a definite Power that we personally can tap into. I'm deeply feeling concentrated Power with this, in a way that I did not in the other rituals. I am reminded of the big heavy street rollers that level a pavement... this Power is such that nothing can get in its path, there is no question of resisting the gold that is coming off of this energy. It is consuming everything before it that should not be there and purifying what isn't consumed (like the burning bush). Goodness energy is purified and amplified, the lesser is simply consumed by it. Similar to the way darkness disappears when you turn the light on...just no question about it...it just simply no longer exists in the Light.

7. I also sensed that some tremendous, huge energy that has been anchored in South America for 26,000 years, transferred in this ritual from there to North America. This, in that the Beings of this continent and Canada are moving at an increased rate from the flame of this golden circle that has been anchored here. This is because enough of the individuals who had been anchored the One God Consciousness in the South American areas, are trying to incarnate some of their people up through Mexico and on into the southwestern border areas of United States. I also felt strongly that the four persons conducting this ritual, have a part in this movement to reincarnate these people.

8. I feel Tuella's energies in the northeast, and I feel Lourdes energies in the southwest of South Africa in their past lives, and a pulling together as it were. Many of the high priests and priestesses who were born in those older civilizations came to help them. I feel them coming through again reawakening that energy within the darker skinned persons of our country...for so many religious movements that express in our country address the white man's religious needs, and I see some leaders coming through who address the spiri-

tual needs, and I see some leaders coming through who address the spiritual needs (not religious) of the Spanish, Negro, Oriental Americans, also Polynesian Americans...a whole group of people being overlooked. Some colossal Flame, or Seal has been brought from South America and moved up into North America where great spiritual awakenings will happen in the United States, Canada and Mexico.

9. I also saw that the Avatar of the northeast, coming together with the Avatar of the southwest in this important ritual, would manifest a very ancient healing between two races of beings able to see beyond the illusion of racism, therefore I would suspect that we would see some healings of racism in the area, similar to Martin Luther King who came out of a ministry that had a political impact upon this time. This time the cycle will be completed without violence, but by a leader who will be loved by all sides, because of his spiritual love and beauty.

10. I also saw that the great Golden Seal would now make it possible for Beings who had never incarnated on this planet, to now begin to come, so that we will begin to see young men and women sponsoring children with incredible integrity. It's like a Golden Doorway has been created for highest beings to come from even other Universes, through that area. The great Golden Doorway has been created for highest beings to come from even other Universes, through that area. the great Golden Seal has eight suns upon it, like an immense Mayan calendar, and it invited eight levels of beings to come in and be here on this planet at this time to help the planet get through its difficult time of transformation fully into the New Age. Beyond that, when that work is completed, then they would gather this specialized group and take them back with them into the Cosmos once more. I feel that these eight energies coming in from eight universes, who sponsor the eight races, represent four who are women and four who are men, anchoring their energies within the planet.

11. Apparently Tuella and Lourdeas are the first born of two great Kings and two of these Golden Beings are King fathers from Universes really very far away, and these are connections made a very long time ago. The eight concentric circles, the eight golden suns, are coming off the energies of your arms for some reason. And these circles are just there to push back any form of obstacle that

would obstruct the coming in of these eight Beings and their helpers. Therefore this ritual had to do with all of these future plans for the Earth and its destiny. Gold was the color of the day."

#5 Long Beach
Part 29

1. Arriving at Long Beach Harbor fairly early, strong guidance was given that we were to stay at home that day and together study all of the material accumulated thus far in the Father's Throne messages received up to that time. The discussion was intensive, lengthy, lasting four hours, productive and unifying in the group understanding of the Father's messages.

2. In the quiet peace of that evening looking across to the Long Beach mainland, we completed the powerful ritual for the entire Los Angeles area, from a high balcony. the date was August 27. The following day Lourdes experienced a temporary illness which confined her to bed, but it was just the space needed for her to spend in study and meditation upon all of the Father's writings and the discussions of the day before. This was important for her, for she has accepted the responsibility and commitment for the dispersal of the Father's material throughout the country of Mexico.

Back home, ELLYSSA had recorded this enlightening vision:

3. This time the metaphor shown to me was a silver armed cross. At its center, it is so very silvery it looks white to me. At the outer edges of the arms there is an effervescent marbleized appearance in the silver, and the end of the arms comes to a three-pointed tip, similar to the Roman Cross. This time the four individuals at the ritual are not holding hands, but still in their circular position, have their arms held out, so that they themselves are human crosses as they face the inside of the circle. There is a pyramid shape at the end of each arm, which is swirling purple, blue and green.

4. We worked with the Father's energy in the Golden Circle but this time we are working with the Mother's energy, that the cross is the anchoring on the earth of the Mother's energy. In the swirling of these three colors it's interesting that these are the three lower female colors of the rainbow. In the Gold, people were awakened to their service to God but in the Silver Cross energy I feel that people are awakened to their commitments to each other, through promises that

111

had been made over the eons, or commitments of long standing. This energy here feels like the individuals in the area have anchored their love, and intuition, and brotherhood, and that this cross is pulling from within them and amplifying the energy so that the four of you aren't having to do it alone.

5. The energy that is being cleaned out of the area is that which would harbor resentments, unforgiveness, jealousy, rivalry, competition, the heavy stuff that keeps relationships from flowing and growing smoothly. It's interesting to me that as I see the four individuals facing inward to the circle and pouring into it, but the fact that their hands are not touching tells me that this is an energy that would require people to work together. Remember that in working with that Gold energy, just one individual could transform a neighborhood, but in this Silver energy, the Mother's energy, that where two or more are gathered and serve Her and have a commitment to the planet Earth and its inhabitants, that they can tap into this Solar Silver Cross.

6. I also had a sense, as I watched the center white silver moving out toward the swirling colors at the ends of the arms, that we are going to see a very rapid increase in UFO sightings. I saw that we begin to see a breakdown in the secrecy wall, the hush hush stuff, that we will actually see the government admitting to it, and see some unusual terms in it. The Cross is the anchoring of the humanity and the Divinity parts of ourselves, so I also have the feeling that we will have more of the proof of UFOs left behind...actually on a very concrete level, we experience the discovery of a NEW METAL, in this very area, from this Cross. And it is interesting that as you look at the Cross, you have these three pointed energies at the end of each arm, which totalled makes 12 points. I had a feeling that if you counted the center point, it would be the 13th one, the secret, as it were. Because this energy will create new scientific information for the human race genetically. Some secret that will prove the human race did not leap from one source but has several sources which have come from several parts of the cosmos. A most interesting breakthrough.

7. I sensed a hungering for the feminine aspect of the Godhead. Even though the Mother has always been referred to as the Holy Spirit, it has never been consciously recognized that this aspect is

actually a Mother's energy of this Triune Godhead.

8. This Cross feels really active. I feel something important in each of these 12 points. In one point, I can see the UFO activity increase, as well as the belief in it. I see the discovery of the new metal, and I see the genetics research breakthrough. I also see an improvement in the battle of the sexes so called...men and women beginning to hear each other because men are beginning to find the feminine side of themselves. So I felt a softening of the distance between the males and the females of this planet. I see changes in divorce laws even things as simple as that.

9. This particular ritual will take the longest period in full manifestation of its results. I see the 12 points as cycles, so solidly grounded into the human experience. It will actually take 13 months from this day that we see it. It's like I see these points, but it's not until we see the 13th that we see the connection of them or how they affect one another. There's something about what happens at the 13th point, where the two bars cross, that pulls all the other "happenings together.

10. Even though this one is the longest in terms of seeing the results, it actually was the most effective in scattering the carnate and discarnate consciousnesses that do NOT want the planet to evolve. This is because they want to continue to control it with their money, their superficiality, and so on, and there is so much rapid change and newness of thought forms, that they lose their power for that reason.

11. The world has yet to experience the martyrdom of a female saint, and I feel that somehow this is involved in that 13th center point. It's as if the Mother's heart has to be put down in order for her children to value her. Some tremendous female focus of Light will remove herself as a way to anchor or awaken the children's need of Mother.

12. This concludes the thoughts from the metaphor of the equal armed Silver Cross, of the 5th ritual of the Father's cleansing.

#6 San Diego
Part 30

1. The sixth ritual took place on August 28, at Mission Bay, San Diego...Pepe recorded his experience:

When we began the force-field procedures, I felt all of these beings close in and around us. Many, many of the fallen ones from out of the mountains began to enter into the force-field which we were creating for their departure. In the middle of the force-field, a circular Light beam appeared...very, very bright...then it expanded to cover the entire area where we were. The sky above us was thick with ships high up as well as close in near us; just over the water behind us and above the sand before us. A marvelous pink Light began to expand and glow upon all of the area to be covered by this ritual, and I saw all of the fallen ones proceeding into all of the waiting ships in subdued and humble manner. They came in by thousands to enter the fleets that waited. My inner guidance reported that this ritual harvested the greatest multitude of fallen ones they had rescued thus far.

2. It is a fascinating thing that Pepe tells what you would have seen if you were clairvoyant and were on the scene, but in the visions and metaphors received by ELLYSSA, we are told what the cleansing action of the ritual and its consequential outcome in spiritual results released. Within each of these seven visions is contained much in-depth spiritual truth for a group to discuss, and I would strongly recommend to all of you that you make the most of these wonderful visions for your study groups.

Here follows ELYSSA'S vision and report for August 28 and the sixth ritual:

3. The moment I focused in upon this ritual, I saw the four faces of the participants, but they all had the look of babies: just old enough to begin to see some signs of what their adult face will look like. I was then aware that they all had lines of contact with a large pink mass. I felt as if I were inside of an egg. So when I pulled back my vision of them, I saw that they were all enclosed in one large pink egg. The shape of the metaphor today is like an ovoid egg shape, not a circle as others have been, the color of this ritual is emphatically pink. The vision immediately moved from this picture to a softer shade, a pink of newness. It brought to my mind the Garden of Eden or something like that, in that everything was fresh and new and innocent, and back to square one, back to zero.

4. The pink energy from this ritual was lifting off the planet a lot of karma that had been left on it by the human species that have

used it. This was making way for an energy that could awaken within everyone a Garden of Eden kind of energy. The babies I saw shared the same source for their needs, all fraternal twins even though they looked different. Again I felt the repetition of yesterday's Mother energies, but in a much more pronounced intimate way. This particular pink energy would give the most benefit to the four individuals in the ritual, but also this ritual was to effect every child upon the planet under the age of three. Everyone of them would have some of their personal karma lifted so that they could assist in bringing this Garden of Eden consciousness to the planet. In other words, in the Garden, all of the animal life was appreciated, all of the vegetation was blessed, the birds in the air as well as every other being. Therefore little children who may have already been under the pressure of some form of child abuse in their environment will have that burden lessened (not lifted).

5. This new pink energy will also attract more and more young people to the many New Age movements that embody this loving flame. It is, of course, explicitly a heart energy. It is not of the head, not mental, but a living of the ideation of the highest goals rather than just wishing for peace, etc., as the older generation had done. This shall bring Love in ACTION.

6. I felt this pink ovoid that enwrapped the four individuals, begin to throb like a heartbeat. In other words, the color is pulsating continuously, like a cosmic heartbeat of the Mother to her little ones and through the energy that is beamed out. This is the first color that I felt so quickly, and it very quickly encased the whole globe. Each beat of the heart as I am watching it talking to it, goes out for hundreds and hundreds of miles at that radius. Therefore this awakened generation, even though they have their individual development, this generation being born, three and under, will not allow this planet to be harmed any longer, and will immediately start addressing the wrongs done to Mother Earth. We will see real action...not commitment (burial) in committee's.

7. This is the first ritual in which I have heard sound, other than the whispered whooshing of the first one. With this one I am listening to this throbbing of this heartbeat. The greatest gift this pink ray is bringing is comfort, reassurance, "I AM here," "I can help." It's as if a mother went into the room of a three year old and she says,

"Look you have to start cleaning this up." But she kneels down and helps the three year old clean it up. It's quite obvious the three year old made the mess, but its also quite obvious that the three year old can't clean it up by himself either. That is the consciousness I am feeling about the Earth right now, a three year old kind of consciousness with the Mother energy helping us to do what must be done. The child sees some responsibility in what it has done to create the mess, and manifests some willingness to aright the mess, even though he could not possibly accomplish it all on his own.

8. It is such a soft, soothing energy. Not the powerful slashing and cutting of the others; just gentle, loving, like the soft ripples on a lake as opposed to the hard waves of the ocean breakers. I feel this pulsating pink radiation just awakening the hearts within the little children as well as anyone over three, who believes and keeps awake that Mother Flame, will experience a comforting, a lifting of the heaviness. This is an energy that will even affect the sleeping people. people who have not awareness at all that they are even alive. It seems to be a message from the Divine Mother, that 'Everything will be alright.

#7 Imperial Beach
Part 31

1. In the early morning of the final ritual, we shivered and insulated ourselves against the sharp winds of the bottom of the California coastline. I looked southward toward the Baha, and Central America and South America. With a burdened and heavy heart to lead me, in the mind's eye and with the speed of an angel, I travelled down the entire western coastline to the Falkland Islands. I felt a compulsion to expand this final ritual to include it all. This ritual was by no means going to be routine. I realized what such a departure from the afore planned itinerary of the Ashtar Command would cause in confusion and ill-preparedness.

2. Therefore, after our usual pre-ritual program, I called upon the Commanders to alert them of my intention, carefully detailing just where I proposed to call forth the fallen ones. Realizing they could move their fleets around faster than the speed of Light, I gave them 15 minutes in which we would silently wait and requested that we be given the ALL ALERT signal from them when they were posi-

tioned and ready to fulfill my request.

3. During that brief interval, we were all aware of the hubbub I had stirred up. It was like trying to sit quietly in Grand Central Station during the rush hour! We all sensed them running about on the Craft. I could hear officers in consultation with Ashtar, some less seasoned ones were complaining in a nice way that they "weren't ready for that." I heard another say, "there isn't room." I was a bit amused as I listened. But I was determined to sweep the entire western coast of this hemisphere with the Love of the Father to all of these wayward ones. I had also called for extra legions of Angels to be positioned lengthwise over the area of action and then I thanked the Father for His Divine Presence through it all.

4. The 15 minutes seemed like an eternity as we quietly waited and continued to be brushed by the ordered chaos above. Finally, unitedly, we all received confirmation that they were (if somewhat breathless) at last ready to bring off this massive exodus. Lord Ashtar had quickly pulled in all of his fleets from the eastern coasts, the European theater, and far north of us, everything was ready.

5. Then I began to Call to the fallen ones working country by country along the coastline. We explained to them what was taking place, the reasons, speaking in love to them, beginning with the Islands of the sea, Lower Argentina, all of Chili, Peru, Ecuador, Colombia, Central America and western Mexico. Pepe watched them pouring over us and into the shops everywhere like a cloud of eagles darkening the sky. Squadron after squadron of Angels came with their charges to deposit them into the Craft. At this point, Lourdes experienced an interesting insight. She tuned into "...a strong exchange of love from them to us...those who were going up. At that moment when you told us to hold hands, I saw that all of the beings in the middle who were going up, were not the same as others have been. Their vibration was different. I knew they were Light Beings but why were they here? They were like a group, and they were shouting at us through the force-field, "THANK YOU!, THANK YOU!, THANK YOU!," and waving their hands in Love. There were so many crowded into that pillar of Light, but they were somehow separated from "the others."

6. Pepe had also observed this scene, and had heard them as well. He smiled and waved back, and knew somehow that they were

special ones. Then it was revealed to me that they had been trapped souls, trapped in the thicket and briars and undergrowth. I reminded the others of the scene of a young lamb caught in the thicket into which he has placed himself and he cries to get out and return to his mother but he cannot. The Shephard has to come and cut away the thorns from his being and literally lift him out of it to return him to the flock. That group of souls had become trapped in the thicket, so to speak, that had been made by the fallen ones.

Lourdes had beheld a very beautiful lady in the ascending group who was one of those rescued from the trap as she pathetically smiled and waved her arm and also shouted, "THANK YOU ALL OF YOU!" Personally, within me, my heart felt such a gratitude to the Father for such a wonderful privilege in allowing all of us to be a part of this experience. And I knew that all of you at home also, who had supported this mission our Light, and Prayers, and Love offerings were also an integral part of that rescue along with us.

7. It was all a big sweep, a tremendous operation, and the Ashtar Command was incredible in their smooth handling of an emergency situation. It was well that it was early and the beach was deserted, and cold, because in my enthusiasm my voice rose to the shouting extreme. I had no reason for stopping at the Mexico border, and Love dipped down to Penguin land to gather all of the fallen ones who were willing to leave it all behind and ride off into the sunrise with God...*on His terms!* A triumphant conclusion to an exciting journey.

8. Earlier, on the morning following the first ritual account, I omitted something. As we returned to Santa Rosa, my vehicle decided to self destruct in its transmission just in front of a repair shop in Santa Rosa. It was small and uncomfortable for four persons and all the necessary luggage for so long a period. So a few blocks farther we found a lovely roomy white Lincoln sedan to rent for the Father's mission and thanked Him for the exchange. On this last ritual morning, spent and weary from all of the intense excitement, we hurried off to rack up some miles toward Santa Rosa again, to redeem my fallen charger (for a pittance of $920), and to deposit the nice Lincoln God had loaned us. Thus we headed back to the Sacred City, flying across Nevada like it wasn't there. So dear friends, if perchance you were trying to call the Ashtar Command, early morning

for August 29, and the line was "busy"...now you know why.

9. On that journey home, Pepe saw a Golden Beam on our car with a wide Pyramid at its top high above us. He also saw the scout ship clearly, that always traced our travels, plainly seeing the observation windows with four occupants inside. A message was given concerning the appearance of a Great Being who was coming to be with us, embodied like us. At another time in the car, Pepe had been taken out of body to a city high in the mountains. It was a Master's retreat. Torches of burning fire completely surrounded it, but the other details of the experience were lost.

10. We had been out of touch with my daughters and we were not aware of the wonderful visions and reports of results that had come to them. The following vision of ELLYSSA's 7th ritual meditation was waiting for us.

11. "At first there seemed to be no shape at all. It felt like droplets of something in the air. I felt the Solar Team, so called, being surrounded by a lavender mist. Then suddenly I was aware of trillions of stars in the sky. They began to fall, like raining stars. As I looked closer and caught some of them in my hand they were diamond shaped. This falling rain of higher consciousness represented by the diamonds, belonged to all of the individuals who would be spiritually stirred to awaken that consciousness. I was hearing that this would now be the time when persons who had been incarnated here for a few hundred years off and on, would now be awakened to their mission and reason for being here. We were to expect to see them moving into position in 1990. The lavender seems to have strong extraterrestrial connotations to it, along with Angelic. It represents many consciousnesses, not just one being, or a group of beings. It's like there was a reconnection made on some level between individuals and their guardian Angels, who are committed to their individual well being.

12. The lavender is the most delicate, the most healing, of all the energies right now. You will notice that each consecutive ritual and its certain color or colors has prepared the way for the next color which was to follow. The pink will definitely bring in a lot of healing of psychological nature and emotional balance. Thus now as the lavender shows up, the Angels can come through it and have an opportunity to create miracles in our lives. Especially if it is consciously understood that it is happening. But even if it were not, as long as there is a sign that 51% of a person's consciousness is aligned with what is good for the planet, the Angles can work with the 49% that is not.

13. We will see more rapid development in people, in a shorter amount of time. The lavender is much more cleansing of everything. For example the other colors were specific in their work of cleansing. The lavender mist, with its falling diamonds, is like a general anti-septic for all cleansing purposes; as if the lavender was the last final cleanup to remove any final adverse energy that would get in the way. It will also work great to awaken the intuitive nature of persons so that they can become more aware. Because these diamond stars were falling, it tells me that individuals are inviting more and more, their own Higher Selves to come down and express in them.

14. In this mist, I also hear music: harps, violins, tiny bells; indicating that more of a heaven consciousness can manifest openly after the pink brought in the Garden of Eden consciousness. I know also that enough work has now been done in the rituals, by the team the Father has sent, that now the Angels can process more of the details of His Plan. Individually, for the four principals who participated in the rituals, I sense a deepening awareness of their true individual identities, becoming intuitively connected with their spiritual selves.

15. Therefore, I see that because of the rituals, the stage is now set for a sweeping spiritual awakening not only in the locations of the rituals but throughout the world. Thus ended a series of special releases from the Throne Energies commenting upon this Mission for the Father.

Section 7

The Thirteenth Vortex • The Gulf of Mexico

Where Men Become Gods
Part 32

1. It was not just circumstances or impulse that led the Mayans to inhabit the land of Mayans. Thanks to their cosmological conscience, they knew the land they had chosen to settle in, was sacred. The locations of ceremonial centers were the results of profound beliefs and were built in places of great natural beauty, whose magic allowed them to develop one of humanity's most extraordinary cultures.

2. Thirty miles northeast of Mexico City at Teotihuacan, is the most ancient vision in all the Americas. The magnificent Pyramid, Pyramid of the Sun. A 217 foot summit and a breathtaking view. The classic Teotihuacan construction remains a mystery. It is only known that it was abandoned around 750 A.D. Five hundred years later the Aztecs revered it as "a place where men became Gods," and used it as a ceremonial center.

3. In addition to the Pyramid of the Sun, several other structures have been excavated since Teotihuacan's rediscovery in 1905, including the Pyramid of the Moon and the fortress-like Citadel. Of particular interest is the Temple of Quetzalcoatl. Teotihuacan is Mexico's most famous archaeological site. It is valuable for the links it establishes among the many people who shared its influences from its mysterious Creators to the Toltecs and Aztecs.

4. I had been told that our final briefing and information would be on hand by departure time. We needed to know more but the heavens were like brass and the information hadn't come. We decided to call a special session with the Lords of Light and flood them with questions. Ellyssa (Eve), was the channel for the session. As soon as she hit her chair the information started flowing, and I began immediately with the questions.

WHAT IS THE DEEP PURPOSE IN MY HAVING TO GO TO

YUCATAN?

5. When I view the entire operation that the Father has planned I see the colors purple and gold. You had incarnated on those rays in a time before history was recorded, before Atlantis or Lemuria. There was a civilization of which there are no existing records located in the area that is now beneath the Gulf of Mexico. At one time this land was connected to Africa and a tremendous earthquake split the body of land away from the present coast of Africa. The land mass sank and all that is left of it now is the outer edge of Yucatan right along the coast.

6. You incarnated to implant a technical device in a pyramid which is now under the water of the Gulf. The people appear to be of the 6th root race. They tunneled beneath the mountain and built a pyramid, and within the pyramid constructed a special chamber for the device which you implanted. At that time you promised these people you would return. Because you placed the apparatus there in the past, you must return to the area we know as Yucatan to activate it now.

WAS THAT A DEVICE OR OBJECT PLACED THERE FOR THE PURPOSE OF KEEPING THE PLANET SECURE UPON ITS LEY LINES, AND STEADY WITHIN ITS ORBITING OR SOMETHING LIKE THAT?

7. What I am seeing are these belts of color/energy that were generated from the six rituals on the California coast, and what this device will do is maintain those belts of energy after the Special Invocation is made. I was picking up the sixth root race...they were here even before the giants were on this planet and they're going to return again. The entire land mass fell so there is no record today of these people.

8. That is basically what this action is all about. This tremendous craft that you keep saying has to be brought lower in its altitude and brought down as it were...many of those Beings who are high enough to handle the beginnings, and the basic, at the beginning of this planet, ARE ON THAT SHIP. They are the very people that will begin to incarnate. There is going to be a huge rise in births around the Gulf and Yucatan area, as well as the specific areas where you did the rituals to remove the fallen ones. According to the colors, they come in on, they will be born somewhere on the planet where

that pink band is circling. The rituals and the color band have cleaned those particular areas for those who will be born on that color ray, cleaning it and preparing it for their coming.

9. The reason they have to be here is sunk deep within the water...their interest is not anything on the land but rather what is in the water. The name of the place steps with "H." There it is. I thought it would be protruding out in the water more, HUNUCMA ...That's it! There's something about the letter H, they were showing me H without the connecting line. They told me of the story of Samson in the Bible between the two pillars. He was one of those who was part of that rise. I'm feeling a lot of land upheaval, hurricanes, all kinds of disturbances because that's going to be agitated down here (Gulf waters). Once you complete the invocation it's almost as if you begin to cleanse the land of ignorance...not evil but just ignorance.

WHY DID I PUT THE DEVICE IN THE PYRAMID? CAN YOU SEE ITS NATURE AND PURPOSE?

10. That which you are activating is like a computer chip, or a part of a computer, or a homing or communication device. The computer is on the Great Craft, the New Jerusalem, and this device is perhaps like a modem. The reason you placed it there has something to do with the COSMIC SCHEDULE, and it was placed there as a failsafe device. If the human species had not evolved fast enough to meet the COSMIC SCHEDULE then the 6th root race beings would have to return, incarnate, in order to complete the necessary work at this present transition time. And the species cannot handle the energies, therefore the 6th root race is incarnating. The rituals you completed in August created belts encircling the planet and the Yucatan ritual activates what is like a buckle of the belts. These belts will hold the energies in place, and distribute the energies evenly around the entire globe so that the planet will survive the transition. The 6th root race beings who are incarnating, and a lot are here now, are able to handle the energies, and they are and will be, the leaders, healers, seers, sensitives, and teachers who can lead the planet and the human species into the next phases of development.

11. An earlier attempt was made to anchor these energies through the device which is historically known as the Ark of the Covenant. There are many highly evolved people on the planet at

this time who are awakening to their Christ Consciousness who were involved in that attempt to anchor the energies in the time of Moses. That is why Jesus incarnated through the Jewish people. These people made commitments to the 6th root race, perhaps to birth them now, in order to aid the planet in the changes ahead.

IS THIS DEVICE CONNECTED TO THE GREAT PYRAMID?

12. The image I see is the pyramid with the eye, the image on the American dollar bill. The huge eye has lines radiating, vibrating from the iris. The pyramid is an amplifier of these resonating energies. The sunken pyramid will not be completely activated until the chamber in the Great Pyramid is reactivated, and that which activates it is "intent." Your intent to do that Pulsating from these arcs, partial circles as it were, arcs of pulsations that become farther and farther apart at the farthest distance, but do not run into anything...so when you gather here on the water's edge in the invocation ceremony, your radiating pulsation will go toward the other and will link together and form a bridge. The radiating arcs will connect into this, what I call a Cosmic Belt Buckle. I don't now the scientific term, but it anchors the energies and they move over the land.

ARE YOU SATISFIED WITH THE LOCATION WHERE YOU DREW THE "H" ON THE MAP...HUNUCMA...THAT IS, WHERE THE POINT OF INVOCATION IS TO BE?

13. Yes, and at least there is a good highway going through there. As I said, the letter "H" gives the key to the energy pathway. You are the arc (H), and the two men will be the pillars. You will have more strength to do this activation if the team can stay in the area a few hours. Wear something that is purple and gold, and wear gold in your hair. I'm hearing gold in the shape of pyramids. Wear genuine gold on each wrist and something on the head or neck and it will awaken the old memory of the time before, when you promised you would return. Do not wear any other kind of metals, not even bra fasteners, trouser zippers, or eyeglass frames etc. because other metals will conflict with the energies. You will be using your bodies as energizers and the activation will happen faster without the interference of metals other than gold.

ARE THERE OTHER PYRAMIDS, PLACES ON THIS CONTINENT, WHERE WE SHOULD GO TO MEDITATE?

14. All of the other pyramids are relatively minor spots com-

pared to the one hidden under water in the Gulf. The other pyramids were constructed to prevent the original land mass from crumbling and sinking entirely, for there had to be something left in present time in order for these rituals to be performed. But now the east side of the Yucatan will fall away and there will be many land changes in that area around the Gulf and the Yucatan. The flat area will flip over like a pancake. Indentations on the east coast and on the west coast, at the narrow area, will become a body of water dividing this land strip. This will be over a long period of time. A wide body of water will finally cut this country in half. But new land will appear in the Gulf area. All of the areas which do not have pyramids are safe, secure areas because their foundations did not require special structures to maintain the energies.

OK, AND SO MY PURPOSE IS TO GIVE THE INVOCATION WHICH WILL REACTIVATE THIS CENTER?

15. Yes...you will literally be the eye of the pyramid and the other three individuals will form the pyramid around you by being the three points. I am seeing something to do with the letter "H" (*looks at the map and points to HUNUCMA*). I see the letter "H" without the crossbar and I relate this to the Biblical story of Samson who stood between the two pillars of the temple. His story represents the destruction of the old way to make way for the new. That is what this is all about, the anchoring of the energies of the new way for a new people. This is the end of two 26,000 year cycles, and so these rituals clear the way and prepare very clean land with high vibrations. Samson was the arc (H) between the two pillars. And in this ritual you will be the arc (H) and the two men will be the pillars. The two men are requested to put their hands on your shoulders or on the pulse on the inside of your wrists to ground you. You do not have the strength to do this alone.

16. THE INVOCATION RITUAL is in two parts. First there is the pyramid part where the three individuals form a pyramid with Tuella in the middle. The second part is the "H" formed by the two men as pillars and Tuella as the arch. Lourdes and the two men should also wear purple and gold. Throughout the ritual she is to KEEP MOVING, KEEP BREATHING DEEPLY, EXHALING IN AND OUT IN CONTINUAL MOTION. Lourdes' continual motion is a distraction. That is her job. She is to keep moving, like stirring a

126

pot, agitating the energies and serving as a distractor from what you are doing and thereby protecting you from that which is destructive. Her commitment is to protect the three of you. Lourdes needs to be over on the land side of a large outer circle within which Tuella will do the invocations.

17. Half of the circle will be on land and half in the waters. Therefore stand in as close to the water as possible, and Lourdes is to stay within the circle as she moves about. Stand at the waters edge and face the Gulf, not the ocean. Lourdes is to face the land as Tuella, Pepe and the doctor face the Gulf. She should hold her arms out as she protects you with her back to your backs. She is protecting you from what appears to be dark energies of the Caribbean witchcraft. It is not that this energy has a consciousness, it is simply that it will be drawn toward the Light, and Lourdes has a really large aura and it will be seen by the disincarnate energy and in this way distracted from what you are doing. The ritual will clean up much of the land. In part, it sank because the land was misused. You will activate the generator communicator and the land can rise again.

18. The team is going to act as a human generator and so you will get awfully hot. Dress as cooly as possible and perhaps stand in the water for the invocations. The ritual can be done early in the morning and for the remaining hours you could have a picnic. Rent a large umbrella for shade and be sure the chairs are wood and cloth and not metal. You will be very hungry after the ritual. You will feel tingling and physical sensations. Tuella, you will feel this in your head chakra and the others will experience this on the spinal column. This ritual will be tiring for Lourdes for she will have to create and hold a wall of Light to hold the darker energies back. If you remain there a few hours, it will give the necessary time for the arc (H) to strengthen and thus to firmly anchor the Light.

19. The whole team should experience spontaneous recall of information relative to the shop being anchored, or personal knowledge about yourself or each other. There appears to be something diamond shaped being placed at the nape of the neck. There are personal beliefs to be reaped for having experienced these energies such as revitalization of the molecular structure; hair and nails will grow faster, vision and hearing should be sharper, and cells renewed faster for as long as the next six years.

20. As for the words of the invocation, *it is really intention that matters.* The calling and the contribution of the throat chakra is mostly to strengthen and feed the intent of the team. It is the intent that will bring in the energies for the work to be done. You don't need a call for the land to rise, just call in the City of Light to be closer to the earth to do its work for the planet.

WHY DOES IT HAVE TO BE ME?

21. Because you are the one who planted and installed this modem or communicating device. It reminds me of a part of a computer, like a modem would be to a big computer somewhere else. The Ark of the Covenant that was carried into the wilderness was a very weak attempt to do this but it didn't work. That's the reason Jesus had to come through the Jews because the Arabs were not ready to let him through. This has something to do with the second coming, that is, with people awakening to their Christ Consciousness. So there are a lot of beings that have made commitments to the sixth race that is upon this planet. You're going to see a lot of very highly evolved people being born on this planet, just to get it through what it has to face, and then they won't have to come back anymore because by then earthquakes and such activity, etc., will have pushed this up and people will find what's within it.

22. I am seeing the waters around the invocation as a big eye, open and wide...but over here...the area over here on the Caribbean, eyes narrowed to slits so that you cannot give it good eye contact...and I'm hearing that there is a very strong hold of witchcraft that uses the earth's energy to make their stuff work. I had a feeling that was one of the reasons a lot of this land is going to be lost is because it's been so misused. This activation will clean it up a lot, but the land itself just can't sustain itself there. The land beneath the Gulf was sunk because it held so much energy, so much Light, but this huge piece of land sunk in the Caribbean went down for just the opposite reason, it was heavy, a spiralling down. Whereas the Gulf land with its generator, etc., was a spiralling up. Just as you had made a commitment to return, she has made a commitment to protect the three of you. The support of the two males on either side of you are the actual physical rods. You have to have the presence of both in order for that arc to happen. Your presence is like the catalyst. If you just had the two rods, nothing would happen. It is the combination of the three with your intention. With your mind, you can see this arch leaping across from your energy point to the object to be activated. This pyramid you activate represents communion, literally face to face communication. So this activation and its resulting awakening is a huge master step for the human race.

23. Ellyssa was permitted to see the golden chamber hidden beneath the Gulf waters, where the golden modem was kept. She continued..."With the six bands of Divine color rays that you released in California rituals, I see these bands going around and being connected at the point of this golden generator. Because we as a fifth root race, couldn't have lived on that land, the energy is so intense...but IT WILL PUSH BACK UP AGAIN. It will create a whole new set of islands that will greatly resemble the Hawaiian Islands only much larger. Literally a whole mountain range will rise but the secrets beneath it will not be discovered until much, much later.

24. Then Ellyssa was taken up and guided into the big computer room. She sensed knowingly it was located within the MERK-ABAH. "It was weird, the whole room was done in gold, and all over the computer was in sheeted gold. It reached from ceiling to floor and wall to wall. I knew that it was positioned over the entire Gulf area. One of the important reasons they have been unable to descend is they need the golden modem in operation. They need its reciprocating signals so they can properly place themselves, for the signal serves them as a docking interpreter. Where all of you stand your Light ascends and it will be an indicator to them of where the edge of the Gulf is accurately positioned.

Personally, I would be suspicious of a land mass that had to have as many pyramids on it as this area of the globe. They had to install these to prevent the land from sinking so that your team could come along and work with this one *(points to Gulf on Map)*. All of these areas that have not required pyramids are safe, secure areas because their land didn't require the special under structures involved in safety. There are at least 100,000 persons upon the NEW JERUSALEM, of the 6th root race, awaiting the opportunity to come through.

25. "I'm being told that all of you should retrieve an item from the "Point," a rock, a shell, something that will retain the energies

you raised. Take your crystals if desired for that area will be saturated with your energies."

On the Road Again
Part 33

1. Jesus speaks wisely as we move into departure mode. "The travel miles will present an excellent opportunity for briefings and instructions for the Yucatan mission. By that time, much material will be on hand. We bless all of you in a special anointing, a special expansion and the infilling of your hearts with great joy and a sense of your personal importance to My Plans for Earth. You have all come in at this point in time for this very action and that which you will do from this moment forward, as individuals, as a fourfold unit of energies. I shall have you as my First team to penetrate emergency places for emergency needs and I shall know that it shall be done. My Everlasting Arms surround your Beings with Eternal Love and gratitude."

IS THE DOCKING RITUAL AND CEREMONY TO BE DONE AT THE PISCES MOON, 11TH & 12TH, OR THE ARIES FULL MOON OF 13TH OR 14TH, WHEN THE SUN IS POSITIONED IN LIBRA?

2. It is best to be done on the 13th day of the Aries full moon in the sign of the Libra sun. Do not be confused by any human conjectures about Friday the 13th. This activity is too far above all such superstitions and in the control of the highest levels of the highest rulership of the earth. The Libra Sun backs up the energies of perfect balance on higher levels to the perfect balance of your pairs on the physical level. The energies of Aries blasts in a New Beginning for the Light workers on the planet as the ministry of the anchored Vehicle of Light begins its work from the lower dimension. You four are specific volunteers for this united action portion of the plan.

3. The actual Point of Invocation is within the Yucatan state at the southern water's edge because of the proximity to the edge of the ship's location. It will remain permanently docked at the mouth of the Gulf and above its entirety until Earth's events are concluded. For this is the central access to the entire continent.

4. We are anticipating and expecting full confirmation of the October full moon date as given previously. As this week progresses

there will be greater and more detailed material on it. You are requested, if possible, to go to the area approximately four days, at least three, before the day of Invocation to become vibrationally acclimated to the area, the atmosphere and the Merkaba's nearness. This time will be very helpful for all of you.

5. You will be told which pyramid areas may be intended for meditation spots. You are not sightseeing. This is a specifically designed sojourn of specific spots that are beneficial. It is not necessary nor recommended to wear yourselves out stalking over the routes of the normal tourist. Certain spots will be magnetized in your mind for meditation and expansion of being. Read and study the materials, the maps, and let your Christed Beings draw you to those spots but not as the usual tourist; it is vibrations that you are seeking. *I AM Jesus who speaks for the Lords of Light and the Father/Mother God.*

6. For our very brief stay in San Miguel, our host was "The Old Nunnery." An attendant would manipulate the old wooden gate for every vehicle that entered or departed. It was like stepping into another world of lush, breathtaking beauty in this botanist's heaven. Its green beauty with potted blooms everywhere made you just want to stay, but its reluctant, refractory plumbing made you want to leave with haste. But nevertheless the vibrations win you over. You breathe into your soul the weight of the thousands of prayers impregnated into the very walls of this place of peace.

7. In time, the Nunnery had to close, and now serving as shelter to the weary (!!!) they continue to serve, and we continued on our mission through two interesting places, Vera Cruz and Villahermosa. Villahermosa is, of course, the Capital of Tabasco, a city of fast growing economic importance of 300,000 souls. It is a city of contrast. Oil and archeology has produced a most fascinating place within a state which is otherwise almost untouched. The riches of oil have converted the narrow streets of this former riverport into pedestrian malls paved with pink stone and lined with lush gardens.

8. VERA CRUZ is the most Colonial and important of the Mexican ports with both a Cosmopolitan air and old world charm. Seafood served in the open air has brought the city fame. Seaside restaurants or the sidewalk cafes, attached to hotel dining rooms, are an attraction. However, we made no stops in the area, other than to

make the precarious adventure inland to find that museum.

9. At this early portion of this journey, I was finding it difficult to cope with the effects of this Torrid Zone with its unspeakable discomfort from the temperatures, loaded with humidity.

10. This will be considerably more a meditative occasion rather than the ritual journey was. Then the emphasis was on action; here the emphasis is on stillness and absorption. There are conditions and changes within your total forms that will transpire as you sit in the appointed places; changes within the form and the cellular structure that will be of much benefit, as well as etheric closeness, that will amaze all of you.

11. You must expand your consciousness to literally transport yourselves, as it were, to the Merkaba at each meditation. While your bodies sleep you will be with us there to receive implanted questions to pull much information through your human consciousness. These first days will be a time of much reception of material for later sharing, as well as strengthening the vortexial beam for the day of Invocation, and later sharing. The vibrations will be very clean, very clear and gentle.

12. Therefore, as you make this journey realize that each turn of the wheels is bringing you closer to all that your soul has hungered for and meditations in the vehicle should be used for our sending Light vibrations through your forms throughout the countryside as you travel. Bring your emptied vessels for the Lord to fill.

13. A warning please...please endeavor to eat lightly: only that which is necessary, and much in the juice form. Your heavy eating of the first trip contributed to the illness of all of you. When one is under the power of very high vibrations the body has difficulty in its digestion process with much food, because the blood platelets are magnetized differently. For any high spiritual activity, lighter and less food is desirable for better results. Also, attempt to partake of as few drugs as possible relative to human individual condition.

14. The air of the sea will be good for your forms and if seaside meditations could continue for twice a day, three or four days before the day of Invocation, there would be tremendous results on the etheric level where you all truly live. The adornment of very light pastels or white will assist in the assimilating of the vibrations and the ray that will be upon you.

The Human Drama
Part 34

1. After Vera Cruz, and pointing our "craft" toward Villahermosa, we were all spellbound, tied motionless to the spot, as we all simultaneously stared at a tremendous symbol of a complete Rainbow which shimmered over us. The lush and incredible beauty of the Vera Cruz vegetation nevertheless had not covered all the evidence of black magic so prevalent to the area.

The oppressive afternoon heat forced me to dampen my enthusiasm for the mission for a weak moment, then it was gone. The place felt like the Gulf, our highway and its great body of beautiful, blue, blue water, and I yielded to its mastery. Penetrating the soft pastel grounds of the interior of the state where the most humble of Mayans ever lovingly worked for and worshipped their Great Ones.

2. The rather miserable dirt road was lined on either side with flowers of blazing yellow. Flaming red blooms of Campana Bells adorned every little yard. I felt so much love for these ladies who cared for their thatched roof homes. The luxurious, softest, pure white percales *(like a polyester cotton)* were also transformed by their loving hands. These gifted ladies modeled their garments on a yoke top, which had been previously covered with a mass of pastel assortment of color before assembling. One would see these dramatic, white, blooming embroidery creations everywhere, displayed with pride, in the state of Yucatan, on bodies of all ages. Lourdes and I took a moment to enter one of these beautiful little stores to look at lovely white kimonas endowed with the flowers some loving hand had so tediously created, and then handsewn, six inches wide, pure white beautiful lace, everywhere the scissors had been. To this day, I have not wished to soil them in the wearing. They are snow white prayer robes primarily. But the local ladies wear them for all purposes, including shopping.

3. The precisely placed silk knit scarfs to warm the neck and head when the day is new and the night touch still lingers, are placed on the shoulders for precise adjustments for the head if needed. In the front, they are overlapped in great care to form a hammocklike container for an infant. Occasionally we observed local homemakers hand washing their laundries in the creek or river where water would

be more plentiful. We also enjoyed watching the "pork on the hoof" strolling along the dirt roads with no fear of a car, which they seldom see in the agricultural sections. I deeply enjoyed getting to see and meet some of the Mayans of today. They are very short of stature with a rather square facial form. A wide smile is always returned happily from a Mayan, if one will just good naturedly smile, or even if you do not.

(Scenario—Father and Tuella)

4. Father, somehow now, I feel that something tremendous has jelled at this point in Your Schedule. In this square of Lourdes, Myself, Pepe and Dr. Lozano seems so final, so complete. The foundation of a Pyramid is a perfect square. I feel that we four are somehow interwoven in the Ascension Plans of Mexico.

5. My Daughter, I AM WITH YOU within your being, in your thoughts, in your imagination and in your conclusions. I place My Thoughts within your mind, in the pathway of your realization, for you to discover, to accept, to bring into your All-Knowingness. Now hear this My Child, for this is your personal information and important to your coming days. The perfect squaring of MY Energies in Mexico will be in bodies and flow through this Perfect Square of *four from My Throne. These four have united their energies again and again in many settings, in many different times, but always for My Purposes and for the anchoring of My purposes and plans of My Will on Earth.* These four, these two perfect pairs are of My Creation and My Planting for this moment in time.

6. It will take the combined blending of these four energies to bring into the reality of this dimension My Divine Plan. For not only the region of Yucatan but globally for all people. That which has been so heavy on your heart these many days...*BELIEVE IT MY DAUGHTER, BELIEVE IT ALL. Absorb it and place the reasoning mind aside.* Accept these things you have received. This collaborating Throne energy will pull into reality the preparatory work to manifest MY PLAN when the null zone has been accomplished. These fourfold energies must be together in absolute and total harmony...in purest of Love for one another. My Holy City or Tabernacle as John terms it, will indeed be with men. But in the area of its space, this energy of Love fourfold and balanced and in total harmony...in purest of Love for one another. My Holy City or Taberna-

cle as John terms it, will indeed be with men. But in the area of its space, this energy of Love fourfold and balanced and in total harmony of two perfect pairs as a fourfold compass Star, you will travel together to that appointed place for prolonged meditation upon these things I have spoken concerning the presence of the Great City. Bring its realization fully into your beings in purest Love. Pull it down to its lowest positioned placement to be anchored for its great Mission. *THIS MUST BE ACCOMPLISHED.*

7. FATHER: This reminds me of the situations in a Master's Chess game. One begins to move various men long enough ahead to position them in a coordinate situation for a grand move toward a tremendous finale.

8. This is an excellent analogy of My Motivations over a long period waiting for that grand finale of which you speak, which does also interfere with your four present experiences. When your fourfold energies, representing the equal-armed cross, surrounded by the circle of My Love, is positioned for its work, you Tuella will be standing in the middle of a triangle made by the other three. Tuella will give the call while the others contribute power to the situation. Visualize the Great City and its location. Realize it is as wide as the Gulf itself. Our Great City floats up these, influencing everything on the continent below it. Following your Spoken Words, while surrounding it with Love, pull it down to its docking position. It could not an-swer this without the activating Power of the Golden Generator within the hidden Pyramid, within the hidden mountain of the Gulf of Mexico.

9. Tuella, know that we walk every step of the way with you. Your trip to Mexico will be a very difficult one for your physical form. Please bear with us in knowing that your presence in that region is highly necessary for the combined mission involving planet earth. We suggest that you allow yourself much time for rest. You will need it more than others.

10. You are leaving at this time to support this process of change. You will know more of this while you are there. Your spirit body has an active function in these coming events and thus the reason for your inquisitive nature regarding these subjects. (Jesus the Christ)

11. Our group had agreed to meet at the quaint little historic

villa of San Miguel near Queretaro, straight across the Gulf from the point of docking, at Yucatan. The journey southward followed the Gulf Coast.

Merida—The White City
Part 35

1. The famous WHITE CITY, seen from above, is green. It is distinguished by its laurel trees from India, the raymones, the flamboyanes, the cebes and its gold rain tree. However, one does not always come across all of this vegetation that is seen from the air since it is mainly concentrated in the northern part of the city. At one time, MERIDA was also known as the city of Windmills. Water was so scarce, wells had to be dug and prayed for, and the water was extracted by the use of the windmills. MERIDA was built on flat rocky land, well planned.

2. MERIDA IS VERY OLD. It dates from January 6, 1542, when a group of Spaniards who had conquered YUCATAN, founded the city in the ancient THO surrounded by five hills, according to where Don Francisco de Montejo (El Adelantada) had chosen. The plans used the original location of the mansions that had belonged to the principal founders of MERIDA. At the same time, places were allocated for the most important buildings; the Cathedral facing east; the royal houses to the North; the meeting west to west, and Francisco de Montejo's house to the south. All of these buildings will stand and form the Yucatans and form what they call Big or major Plaza. Cathedral construction began in 1563, and was completed 1598.

3. Merida's cathedral had a magnificent main altar and extremely valuable side altars. However, these were destroyed during the Revolution and since then, the front of the altar is adorned with a gift from Spain, a huge crucifix measuring more than ten meters high. In 1605, King Phillip III, conferred upon Merida the title of VERY NOBLE AND LOYAL CITY.

4. Pepe received a message on the day of our arrival at Merida: "Welcome to your home my Friends. We are speaking in an awareness and concern for your physical bodies. We know all of you are tired. We have been monitoring all of you during the trip. Now you are on the threshold of the work. This is when we need you the most.

We will be watching very closely. You will not receive any special guidelines. Lourdes knows the kind of rituals used for the end of a cycle on earth. It is necessary to perceive the area as a vortex.

5. The Cities of Chichan-Itza, Hunucma, and Uxmal, form a triangle on the land. It is recommended that you visit those places. When you arrive there, avoid the roads that tourists are prone to use. Go within and perceive the energy. Plan for a meditation at Chichan-Itza. At this point, Pepe had a vision of something like five posts that were going to be activated.

6. Place all of your intention on this because you have been brought to earth to start the mechanism that will trigger that which follows.

(At this time, Pepe felt, very powerfully, the vibration of Ashtar who was speaking.)

"Do not weaken my friends. The Great White City is awaiting your call. We need you. We know that you have arrived in Merida. We see your Light as a Light House. Our ships are always with you. The Solar Cross Unit will be working from this point, on a daily basis of instruction, in very close conjunction with the New Jerusalem. We will send forth Bulletins and personal directives. This has all been appointed and set into place when your Higher Selves have joined us in conference on this floating City. I AM ASHTAR."

7. The members of my team, being all natives of Mexico, felt little discomfort from the ineffable heat, the relentless humidity. I entered the inferno totally drained on all levels of my reality. I understood why I had been warned by the Guardian to rest and refresh myself every opportunity that was presented. I was confined to total rest for a three day period after we arrived, but I was reminded once again that I wasn't there as a tourist anyway. These rest and retreat days had been built into the itinerary for my benefit.

8. The others carried on, feeling tugs to visit certain places, and they would bring me a recorded report of any occurrences as necessary, which are included elsewhere in this report. They had a strong spiritual compulsion to visit nearby ruins of Progresso, Uxmal Chichan Itzan.

9. The next morning early, they left for the journey to beautiful Progresso. I entered into a day of meditation and reflection and a deep study of instructions to date:

This is my message to you this day, My Daughter. There will be more on this. Think of your fourfold energy cortex as a Solar Cross Symbol. With a firm stick, or anything similar, draw a circle on the ground for the foundation of the ritual, and protection, throughout exchange of praise and thanksgiving. Touch the Celestial area by name and announcing of purpose.

10. *Secondly, within the same circle, the other three shall form a pyramid pattern within the circle, and you, Tuella, shall stand at its center for the purpose of the Invocation of the "Docking for the Great City. The others shall be three columns of strength during that call."*

11. *Thirdly, remain still within the circle for the revolving of the Love Flame for the final boosting of the call and its completion. You will have all hands interlocking at the back of the necks and flow the vibration to the left, round, and round, through the arms energies, to receive revelations or insights that may follow, close, in much thanksgiving and pledge of Love to one another.*

12. *The part that the foursquare energies play in this anchoring is momentous in its broader application. This revelation is for that same purpose within the souls of you four, who are the chosen ones, for this task. The empowering of Love, balancing, and purifying the quadrupled energies, is a vital force for completing My Plan. For all of you it will take a certain amount of blending to be totally united in this mission you face. That which you must do is a bit like your expression, "X marks the spot." Where the team will stand calls for very necessary components of the procedure. The realizations and manifestations shall all soon be with you, My Child, and you shall no longer have to walk by faith but you shall know with an all-knowingness of these things. You will come to see that the togetherness of this Solar Cross Team began a long time ago in detail, on schedule for this moment in time. I Bless you with My Presence and leave you My Love for your day. I AM the Creator and Manifestor of all that is and ever shall be.*

A Visit to Progresso

13. Progresso is 23 miles north of Merida on the ocean front. I had heard such wonderful and exciting things about Progresso. In the past, it had been the main fishing port on the peninsula, but it is

now noted for its inviting palm lined beach on the northern coast, with its beautiful water. It is said the water is so lovely in its color blue, so absolutely clean you can see clearly to the floor, and see your hand deep into the water and see every line. I would have truly enjoyed Progresso, but inertia and illness still had its way, and I was fast losing my battle with it. I was reacting badly from the drinking water, through the other areas, as some of the tourists do. All do not, but I had also taken on some influenza which hit hard when I had little left for the combat. But the team brought home a tape concerning their experiences for the day. It begins with the voice of Pepe as they proceed on the journey:

14. *Today is Monday, October 9, and we are going toward the ocean and Progresso. The primary activation for this trip is to give a powerful call to all of the Hosts of Heaven to increase the Light frequency for this entire Gulf Area. This petition for help from the Solar Cross Team focuses on all of the work we have been sent here to do in the docking of the Great City, "New Jerusalem."*

We have arrived here at the City and we all feel within our Being a very peaceful vibration in this lovely and attractive small town. We are now approaching the shore where the vibration is very gentle and comforting and we feel its Highness. Now we sense the Presence of High Entities walking with us, surrounding us. We continue walking toward some inviting benches at the edge of the sea and there we begin the meditation. We called to all the Guardians of the Light work, extensive to all the areas of the Gulf of Mexico, including the United States territory.

15. *Since we have arrived we have observed a beautiful rainbow. It is very unusual because it forms a Light Pillar of beautiful colors, not in the usual arch form. We were all amazed at the incredible cloud formations. We all sensed the spaceships covered by those outstanding cloud forms. The presence of the Hosts of God was very clearly surrounding us. We paused for stillness and Lourdes began the Invocation.*

16. *In the name of God and the totality of His Manifestations in this existence, in the name of this Solar Cross Team, I Lourdes, from Progresso City, after 12 years since my last visit, have returned to this sacred spot to offer an invocation and invitation to all of the Great Ones of Celestia, the Guardians of Light in the Sea; all of the*

139

Guardians of the Pyramids, the mountains, the valleys, and all of the area of Yucatan and its Light groups.

17. *"We come, Mother Earth, to tell you that we have returned, now there is no danger, it is stime for the awakening, time to come back home."*

Pepe continued to record: We were all deeply moved by a wave of Love for Mother Earth. Lourdes knelt down to kiss the Earth and a hug too; it is incredible how that energy is being experienced. As she does this ritual, a sudden and strong wind overtakes us. The sensation that we felt at that moment was overwhelming. We also saw how one of the cloud formations became a hand. We felt that it was a symbol brought by the Angels. We experienced a sense of answer from them telling us:

"We are here with you, listening and being near your Light. A strong wind of Unity in the higher realms for the work you have yet to do."

18. At this moment I had a vision to me. Light, White Pillars in the center of the Gulf waters of a huge size. I cannot interpret these columns that are coming from the Gulf waters, but Lourdes speaks also of the strong unity that is there and its great collaboration with us. We all regretted that Tuella was unable to be with us but all things are in Divine order.

Lourdes speaks now:

19. This petition was for all of the Light Beings upon the Earth, our Space Brothers, Mother Mary, Lord Jesus, Lord Kutumi, Lord Michael; to all of the Alliances of Women of which I am a member, I also wish to say that Progresso is as I dreamed it would be. I have always had the intention to return at least one time more, in this life-time, if possible. But I scarcely could believe that once more I would be with these people, its Lighthouse, its beach. I really feel I stand at the gateway of home. It was my intention to return to live indefinitely with these friends of the Solar Cross Team. Sorry, Tuella, you cannot be with us today. Be it known that she is my Beloved Sister Cosmically in origin, and soul sister in life since repeatedly from times long ago. I say to Mother Earth also, that we Love her and that we are all here; that we are awakened; that there are many of us here to help to realize our Love; that we are all going to do our part. We are conscious that there is a Divine Plan for us. In good will and

action we shall work for the plan for earth."

Pepe records for us his departing thoughts:

20. As we return to the truck we observed that in this precise moment, the beautiful rainbow is disappearing as if it were drawn away by the upper worlds. It began to rain as we arrived at the truck. Our hearts were filled with joy when, at that moment, we had a vision of a great pyramid positioned behind a cloud, all of a violet color, a very deep violet. This was a great show for us, to see this in conjunction with an indescribable sunset for the ending of our beautiful day.

21. Other well known features of Chichen Itza include its ball courts, the site of day long ritual games, in which the winners were sacrificed. El Caracol, the observatory from which the Mayans traced the paths of stars and planets which they believed determined their fate.

• • •

22. On their excursion to Chichen Itza, which was a long drive taken the day before our day of the invocation ritual, once again Pepe recorded their day for all of us:

"As we arrived at the ruins, we had a spectacular view of the immense Temple of KuKulcan. We all sensed pulsations resonating from it. This was an initial visit to the spot and our astonishment was genuine. We entered meditation at the temple spot, to pull out the energies from it and scatter them throughout the peninsula. The sensation from the pyramid awakened some old memories. We realized that the place was already deeply familiar to the soul.

23. Now Lourdes speaks, "...Some days ago, we were told to follow our impulses from within, that might come to us. The first impulse I feel here is to give a big hug to an enormous tree that is near the area of the main pyramid. It is beautiful, very, very old...I feel the tree and we recognize each other. After I've hugged the tree, I feel a necessity to say to that tree, 'I'm here, hug ME.' I feel this tree is a part of me and I a part of it. It has been many, many years since I...the four of us perhaps, have been in this place. The sensation is like being back 'home.' Now I ask the tree to cleanse and purify my energies because I am going up to the Temple pyramid. I feel a very deep Love for all the world and Chichen Itza. We pause on the steps to create a powerful invocation to the Lord's Hosts. The energy as we approach this area is strong with a good vibration, but as we ascend the great steps it is greatly intensified. We experience the Love of the Father through us. Reaching the upper portions of the Pyramid we rest ourselves. We realize how the Pyramid was pulsating, like a heartbeat. We speak to the Pyramid energy to say, 'We are here, we have returned to you and want you to know that we are awakened. Bless us with your energy and Light. Bless Tuella in the stillness of her room as we all prepare for our Mission tomorrow.' The Great City of Light, the New Jerusalem, is near now. She is waiting like the bride for her groom. You need to be ready, full of love. We come to tell you that now is the time. There is no danger, everything is in Divine Order."

24. Lourdes ended her speaking. They observed some manifestations in the sky. Heavy thunder had exploded above, and all over the place it rained heavily; a strong raining down of Love as if answering their call.

The Chicken Itza Experience

25. The structure is a 75 foot pyramid topped by the Temple. Every architectural feature of the pyramid seems mythically significant. It can be assumed this pyramid represents the Mayan calendar. The steps are representative of the seasons. Each side has steps, multiplied by four equals 364 plus the platform step giving the 365 days for the year.

26. During the spring and fall equinox, the afternoon sun creates a shadow effect on upper Temple steps of a serpent descending the stairs. Looking at only one face of the pyramid, one can see that there are nine corners on each side formed by the nine superimposed platforms. Adding two of these sides, we get 18 which were the months of the year.

27. Each month has 20 days, 18x20 equal 360, plus one "ill fated" month of five days for a grand total of 365 days: the vague year calendar. The 52 sunken panels, found on the pyramid, represent the number of years in the Mayan cycle. Concerning the shadows from the sun, descending the stairway, is the grand metaphor of the descent of the "serpent" god Kukulkan to Earth, as the Mayans conceived it.

28. At this time, also, Pepe began to experience a vision of an "energy connection" being formed between all of the buildings there. This net of energy between the structures was created from the activation that was accomplished through the calls made. Pepe said that when he touched the walls of the pyramid, he could feel the pulsations as clear as his own heartbeat. He tuned into the very core of the Temple where there was a "whirling vortex of white energy."

29. Then Lourdes retrieved the microphone to share this: "During these several days of waiting for the docking ritual, we have all noticed that our souls are being stirred and prepared on higher octaves for tomorrow's work. Our emotional bodies are being transformed tremendously. Sometimes we confused some of the sensations we have experienced. At times it all feels like some kind of human transition, with difficulty in defining our feelings. We have all had flashings of ancient memories of these areas. Some of the veils have been lifted. It is as if all of our lives, our efforts, our pathways, have focused, or were directed toward this moment. We know that, as individuals, we have individual missions. But now together we are fulfilling something we came here to do. Every moment consciousness is being raised. We do not know exactly what will occur tomorrow, but all of us are as ready as we can be to face it."

The Day of the Invocation
Part 36

1. On the day of the docking, that morning, I awoke with a wonderful feeling of well being and much anticipation for our journey. I was feeling ever so much better and ready for the day's events on all levels. As we all gathered for breakfast, there was great joy and Love overflowing through each of us. The waiting had been long it seemed. We shared many things with each other. Pepe had received a very clear message from Lord Ashtar at 8:00 AM.

2. "We are very pleased with the work you have accomplished until now. We know where you are. We are observing you. Everything from on high is ready and prepared for the call and the momentum. The connecting vibration with the New Jerusalem is very strong. We also experience a great sense of urgency for this call to be completed."

3. At this point in the contact, Pepe was shown the Gulf waters

and their tremendous vibrations: "It was overwhelming. There is a kind of celebration in the realms of the White Mother Ship. I can hear their voices and feel their joy. It looks as if thousands of ships from a great distance have come to assist and watch the 'show.'"

4. We are only waiting for the momentum to rise, and your physical presence at the point of invocation. Your presence must be at that spot, for an electrical arch will be constructed there to be connected with the buried Golden Pyramid from the spot where you will stand. The arch is necessary to inaugurate the activation. The results of our ministration to your physical forms is very good. Your bodies are ready. It is important that you do not overeat this morning, so the digestive process will not interfere with your focus, permitting all energy of the physical to be directed to the mission at hand. As you travel, visualize your bodies as suns, emanating Light from the inner to the outer part of you. Then totally relax yourselves and do not use your mind, just allow yourselves to feel intuitively. You need to do this until you reach CELESTUM. When you arrive at your point of beach, again still your minds and wait until you feel prepared for the ritual. It does not matter what happens, do not become distracted. The Lord's Hosts are going to construct a resonating wall to send the energy from the pyramid in the sea, to the New Jerusalem, using the four of the Solar Cross Team as intermediaries. All of Our energy and power will be surrounding your Team. May the will of God be manifested. We Love You and guide you with Our Blessings. I AM ASHTAR and the Command overshadows A Great Day for Mother Earth."

As instructed, we drove in silence. Lord Jesus the Christ whispered to me on the way:

5. "We will be very gradually opening up to your human consciousness a clearer recall and various other gifts. As you linger near the point of Invocation, if possible, we will be able to accomplsih more with your physical vessels. The point of Invocation will become a sacred site in its own right, so it shall be at that certain place the mark of the Solar Cross shall be left in a permanent manner, to mark that place where Heaven and Earth become ONE to position this Mighty City over the Yucatan Peninsula and the Gulf of Mexico.

6. "From this place, its resonating and circulating blessings will

encircle Mother to preserve her forever. For there, at the Earth's center, will sit the heart of The Mother, the heart of The Father, just as you have figuratively pasted a Golden Heart on the wall map before you, in the center of the Gulf. Into this pulsation of the Land of the Dove, the Land of the Brotherhood, will all souls be drawn who are destined for the Coming Journey of Spaceship Earth *Into the Beyond the Beyond.*"

(For many reasons, we were unable to manifest some of these requests, but it can still be done by another in our place.)

7. As we continued down the road to Hunacma, I mused within myself concerning the "coincidence" of our P.O.I. being in a place called Celestrum (place of the Celestrial), and our base, Merida, being called "The Great White City." I thought also of the evening at my house many months ago when Ellyssa said, "It has something to do with an "H," then upon examining the map found it...And now here we were.

8. I learned about ten days ago that ancient Mayans honored the sacred "H" religiously, like the "T" and the "G." Further in this treatise, it was explained that in the ancient teachings *HUN* was the Name for God. So, when Ellyssa pulled up an H and then found H-U-N (uchma) on the map, she was certainly on the button with our guidance.

The Point of Invocation

9. We drove on with a sense of spiritual responsibility, thinking only of our mission. The only thing in sight was a rusty and dilapidated pick-up truck farther down the beach. He was shoveling a load of sand into the truck. He soon departed and we hurried to park closer to the shore and unload our gear.

10. On these remote shores of fishing villages, tiny, almost unnoticeable, we spotted only an occasional fisherman busy with his nets or the motorboats, on the far horizon, going back and forth busily watching the nets. The setting for our day was just sun and sand, at the farthest end of the shore. Our hearts pounded within us as we pierced the morning fog to find the center of the Gulf; looking upward also knowing that throng above us was watching every move.

11. Lourdes opened arms wide, and you would have thought

145

she was going to fly over to the pyramid! Personally, I was amazed at how well I felt. I felt great, great, and was most anxious to get on with the ritual. We chose the exact spot, and the other three found the large sticks (as Father had instructed) and began to deeply outline in the wet sand an eight inch circle. This ancient symbol of the presence of God was an exciting moment to experience. Everything was different inside that circle. The frequency higher, a peaceful circulating, blowing of a gentle vortex began to form. We remained by resonating in clockwise direction, allowing the circular vortex to touch our feet, ankles, legs, torso, and upper areas, and yielding ourselves until the Divine swirling, circulating wave had created a force-field of tremendous power. Then from within that power the Team joined me in the nine sacred O'ms. The effect of this upon us was incredible. Then individually, we each gave our personal prayer of thanks and petition. It was a glorious moment. And now it was time for the Invocation.

12. As we gave the United O'ms, a dome was formed above us. The vibration it surrounded us with was marvelous. The sound of the O'ms was sealed within the dome beyond understanding, as if we were in a closed room as we sent our petitions higher.

A yellow ray of energy was formed in the center of the circle. When it ascended above us, it formed an antenna so our space friends would know where we were. The entire area was filled with uncountable yellow gold starts. This rainfall of the stars inside the circle was totally different from the outside of the circle in vibration. I now indicated that we would proceed with the ritual. We positioned ourselves as the Father had requested. Lourdes was in the front facing the sea. Dr. Lozano and Pepe were behind me and I stood in the triangle center. We remained in this location until all had begun to pick up the pulsing vibrations of the Golden Pyramid which was in the center of the Gulf of Mexico. After we experienced the pulsations we sent back our Love and our energy so we could form the arch of contact with the Golden Pyramid.

13. We faced the Gulf as I proceeded to give the call. Our position at this precise moment was the Solar Cross symbol, with Lourdes facing the gulf and back to us. The two males stood one to my left hand and other to my right hand, and I stood directly across from Lourdes, but she faced the Gulf. As I faced the Gulf, Lord Jesus

told me that where we stood beside the water, was the point where My Being had entered this land for two cycles of time.

14. The call was smooth and powerful and no effort at all. I called for the Water Spirits to reveal their Secrets. I called for the mountain God of the Pyramid Mountain, that must rise, to do so, according to the Will of the Father. I petitioned the Great Central Sun to be prepared at that hour to transfer the belts of colored Light bands. We thanked the entire Hierarchy and Hosts of Heaven to maintain these important color bands that were initiated in the California rituals.

15. An Invocation for the removal of THE FALLEN ONES, one of the Mexico areas, was given. I explained the Divine Indictment to them and requested their departure. I asked that New Jerusalem and the Ashtar Command be prepared now to Generate Their Crafts of Light rays so that we may build with them the Electrical Arc and by using our bodies as intermediaries, pulsate it to the Pyramid and ACTIVATE THE HIDDEN GOLDEN DRIVE. WE WILL THIS TO HAPPEN UNDER THE ORDER OF THE FATHER.

16. Then I addressed 100,000 souls of the 6th root race, who await the open door, and told them what was taking place. I spoke with the "observers" who came to watch, and then assist, in this activation.

17. I spoke further to the entire band of Earth Volunteers, Commanders and Light Workers. I spoke to their Higher Selves, so they would understand what is involved in the docking of the New Jerusalem.

I called for Lord Ashtar to indicate if they are now ready to Lower the Great Craft. I called for the opening of the Pyramid in Egypt to reveal its secrets. We join hands here from the land of the Dove to release the energies that have been held back for many reasons. Then I spoke with the Great Ship, and I spoke with the Golden Pyramid within the deep waters. And then I called upon all of Heaven to help the Great Craft as we invoke its lowering, its positioning within the territory of the Earth's atmosphere. We will also Invoke the reactivation of the Golden Generator beneath the water. I revealed who I was and why I was sent.

18. The team was thrilled with the power of that moment, and in that moment we all knew IT WAS DONE. I could hear the great

shout that came down…"from up there." It was like a deafening roar. Beloved Father, Beloved Divine Mother. Beloved Ashtar and all the Great ones who have come so far…Beloved Children of Light… IT IS DONE! ALL Vortexes are open. LOVE IS IN CONTROL.

19. Pepe gives a report of their experiences during the Invocation. This has been recorded in Spanish, and the tape translated into English by Dr. Lozano, edited and typed by Tuella…quite a round, but we do appreciate Pepe's spiritual gifts. Pepe speaks:

20. "At the beginning of our contact, it was such a beautiful moment. Lourdes and Tuella raised their arms, palms opened to Heaven. I saw from the head of Lourdes, a white energy sphere coming from her coronary chakra. When Tuella raised her hands a Light Beam was formed and sent to the Pyramid speedily, like a chain reaction. Later in the Invocation, I saw arch's were formed of a bright but pastel pink. I had the inner realization that collectively where we stood, we were the post to be created, and the hidden golden Generator within the Pyramid was the other post. The Pyramid was sending out arches of energy, but it was too weak and ineffective. But the one we attached to it began a continuous strong rope of energy whose frequency would be strong enough to accomplish the docking.

21. "The next phase we were instructed to do, just before the big Invocation. According to the schedule, Lourdes was to stand at the rear of the circle facing the southern coastline, the Caribbean side, to distract the dark ones. Doctor and I, placed our hands on Tuella's shoulders, to ground her for the big call. Lourdes shared with us that a group of Angels was telling her what to do, step by step, Lourdes will tell us this:

22. "In that moment, a resonating wall was being created, more than a protection wall. For a few moments, I was able to see this pink wall. But I began to emanate my Love toward our Greatest of All, Master of Masters, LORD JESUS THE CHRIST. I also sent my Love to Beloved Mother of God, and Lord Michael. Then I began to hear the Voices of some Lady Masters, alliances with us. I felt the energies coming from the sea. It was so strong I thought I was fainting. I had instructions about taking deep breaths and then let them go, open your hands, and so on. I have never had such an experience before."

23. Pepe continues: "When we were experiencing the pulsation of the pyramid, I observed how the energy arch was increasing its power gradually. Tuella then asked to know when the Space Brothers were going to be ready to receive the big call for the docking from her and us. After the answer came *(for immediate action)* I could see a triangle building up (1) between us, (2) the New Jerusalem, (3) and the Golden Pyramid in the middle of the Gulf. I sensed the activation taking place. The Pyramid became an expanded vortex of energy. *(Note it had been an idle one before this—T.)* I could see the New Jerusalem gradually turning on its lights like an aeroplane preparing to surface. It was a four-star show to me. The tremendous Craft was moving with oscillating movement. I felt a pull downward accommodating itself somehow. These several things occurred at precisely that moment when Tuella had begun the strong Invocation, and I knew the Docking to Earth within her atmosphere had not only taken place but placed Her so much closer to us. We had been told that the completion of the event would take the Ashtar Command several days, but that Tuella would be informed." (Thank you, Pepe.)

The Return to Merida Home Base

24. About halfway through the occasion, Lourdes was beginning to get upsetting messages from her intuition. She felt that we were in danger and that we should depart the location as soon as it was possible. She consulted the rest of us. By that time, the skies were black and threatening. It was 1:00 PM. We noticed that the ground by the waters edge where we had worked, was now totally covered with water. We had some difficulty getting through Celestrum and back to the Hunucma highway, because the village was already flooded. How thankful we were. We had just barely, by seconds, removed ourselves. Roads returning were also flooded.

25. After we were settled in the truck, and safe from the tropical storm and flood, we then discussed plans for starting north the next day, to put the storm behind us. Suddenly Pepe pulled the truck off the road, and with slightly raised hand, signalled a message was coming through. We entered silence. It was 1:50 PM.

Pepe shared it later with us. "We were on our way back to Merida, having been cut short by the threatening sky, nevertheless the work was finished. I had heard the buzzer sound in my head that always indicates someone is ringing my 'line.' So I pulled off the road quickly. The words came:

26. IT WAS AN INTELLIGENT MOVE TO LEAVE THE SEASHORE AS QUICKLY AS YOU DID. AS A MATTER OF FACT PEPE, I KNOW YOU FELT THE PROMPTING TO DO SO YOURSELF. THERE WAS A REAL NEED TO WITHDRAW FROM THE PLACE BECAUSE OPPOSITION TO YOUR AC-COMPLISHED MISSION WAS ACTING THROUGH THE WEATHER. THERE WILL BE SOME STRONG CHANGES IN THE ENERGIES OF THE POINT OF THE INVOCATION AND LEAD TO FLOODS ON YOUR ROUTE TO MERIDA. WE ARE VERY HAPPY UP HERE OVER THIS GREAT VICTORY. IT WAS A JOYOUS MOMENT AS WE WATCHED YOU INSIDE THE SHINING CIRCLE. ALTHOUGH YOU USED A STICK, THE CIR-CLE BECAME A RING OF FIRE WHEN YOU FINISHED. IT WAS SOMETHING LIKE A TRI-DIMENSIONAL IMAGE OF YOU... LIKE A HOLOGRAM. WE OBSERVED IT ALL. AND ANY PASS-ING DISCARNATE OR BEING COULD SEE THE CIRCLE OF FIRE CLEARLY. THE MOVEMENT OF THE WATER, AS YOU OBSERVED THE RISING OF THE TIDE, WAS AN EFFECT OF THE PULSATING OF THE PYRAMID THAT WAS STIRRING IN ITS ACTIVATION. THESE WERE VERY STRONG PULSATIONS AND EVEN NOW THAT ENERGY IS STILL BEING RECEIVED IN THE LAND THERE. THE FULL ANCHORING PROCESS WILL TAKE SEVERAL DAYS...OF YOUR TIME. WHAT WE ARE SHOWING YOU NOW PEPE, ARE ENERGY WAVES COMING DIRECTLY FROM THE NEW JERUSALEM, THAT APPEAR TO YOU AS CONCENTRIC AND EXPANSIVE WAVES. THESE ARE SIMILAR TO TELEPATHIC WAVES OF TRANSMITTED THOUGHTS.

27. THE ENTIRE GULF AREA IS BEING CLOSED. TWO HUNDRED MILES INWARD FROM THE COASTLINE. THE ENERGY WAVES REACH AND BLESS ALL OF TEXAS TO ALL OF FLORIDA.

28. Lourdes queried the space brothers to determine if we should leave Merida today, or still wait until tomorrow. Ashtar responded that it would be quite right to wait till the next day but

not to delay beyond that.

We thanked our good friend Ashtar, and very relaxed, we proceeded on our pleasant journey back to the WHITE CITY.

Proclamation

By
Jesus The Christ

The 13th Vortex, Golden Power Point, located over the area called the gulf of Mexico, is now activated totally; set into motion for its Mission to Earth.

On October 13, 1989, four representatives of The Throne of God, designated as the Solar Cross Team, gathered at the appointed place, at the tip of Yucatan state to generate this action.

Most will view the date as just a passing day, but when the Solar Team entered the point of Invocation that day unheralded, unannounced, their presence and work in the shadows and the silence, would release in domino motion, the Golden Power of the remaining 12 VORTEXES on the planet.

I PROCLAIM that date of OCTOBER 13TH to be a (HOLY) HOLIDAY for the FAMILY OF GOD everywhere, who LOOK FOR MY COMING AND REJOICE IN THAT DAY.

The experiences of the European people as the desire for FREE-DOM burns within them, is the most outstanding result of the energies released from "docking" and the activation of the New Jerusalem with her sacred place. This type of inner knowledge experienced through the inner senses is not the kind of thing that will penetrate the New Age Movement for at least a year. (Spoken late Oct. '89) But the energies have to begin somewhere and BEGIN THEY HAVE! The penetration of the THRONE INFORMATION finds its way throughout the levels of Earth's realities. Look around you; See it; Believe it!

The next major step will be the implantation of more souls in the stature of Gorbachev in the world-wide political scenario. The changes this man made have been instrumental in inaugurating for mankind will not be totally realized from your side of the veil. His presence on the Planet was a Great Turning Point of international enlightenment. These widespread reform efforts are highly sponsored by the Spiritual Hierarchy and the entering of our Galactic Emissaries will consummate this part of the Father's Program faster than you would imagine. The masters of intrigue and insidious terrorism will begin to dissolve away by virtue of intergalactic intervention. This will release the Light of the World and the call for FREEDOM for mankind will blaze brightly everywhere, when Love is in Control.

War has ended...theoretically, if not actually, in the isolated places. A cleansing of the Military mind is taking place before your very eyes. Social issues move slowly but they will CHANGE. Each step in the upliftment of humanity raises the global vibrations of the mass. It will ultimately lead to that point of no return, in mankind's growth and enlightenment when the triggering status shall be reached. It is then that the fourth dimension shall permeate and integrate planetary life and the New Age. But there will be a moment in time that the planet will need to be swept clean of its clutter. A time for a stillness of planetary life for a moment of Eternity, to resume again its journey, toward its own destiny. Do not give up my friends, the end of things as they have been has already surfaced. The Father's Program for Earth has already unfolded and her ascension is underway. At the foundational structure of human life soon to be visibly realized, our Throne projections have done their work well and that work is almost finished. This has been Jesus speaking for the Lords of Light and the Hosts of God. We Salute You All!

Benediction

By
Lord Jesus and Our Father

This is Jesus, who speaks for the Father and the Lords of Light concerning the Great Joy in the upper Heavens over the Victory of the anchoring of our magnificent floating Kingdom of Light within the atmosphere of planet Earth.

Now let it be understood by Our Children of Light everywhere, that the preparatory stage is now completed. All of the cleansing energies of the Throne of God are now fully active since this activation of the Golden Pyramid in the Gulf of Mexico.

The heartbeat of its inner generator is resonating with our floating World and its colossal computer. All things are now set into position and, since October 13th, Earth world time, change has been the Order of the Day; changing motion to flow to our special emissaries ascension reality.

Quickly, almost immediately in fact, world headlines gave immediate response, as tremendous cries for change arose within the hearts of mankind. In Europe and China hearts were deeply sincere even to the laying down of life itself. To you of Earth, developments across the Continent have been starting. The call everywhere by humanity for FREEDOM is planetary preparation for Earth's Ascension. The anchoring of Earth and Heaven, and the activation of the great Yucatan Power Point has now released every blockage holding back spiritual transformation and individual Ascension.

I report to you that the collective Ashtar Command has been overcome in their duties since October 13th. The total regeneration of the computer contact with Gulf Pyramid has kept them in support to the planet for that which is coming.

On the afternoon you departed from the point of invocation the activation deep within the Gulf water was moving strongly. It rippled and passed through the water quickly and the equipment within the gold computer room of the Merkabah was immediately recording its action. Everything had been made ready there, technically speaking, and with this initiation the Great White City of God is now attached in its own way to the vortex beneath.

The 13th vortex is that one which will rejuvenate all incarnated Light Workers, pouring into their Beings the necessary stimuli to move the balance of the program into its finality. Much has been happening and taking place of which you would not be aware. But you need only listen to the news, look around you, watch for clues, and you will see these things which combine to generate a higher frequency on the planet.

The power of this regeneration will step up up all outpourings of energies to the planet from this source, and at that location. These will, in turn, be carried far and wide, by the encircling belts which were positioned at the rituals on the west coast the month before, as previously explained.

Time has fully brought into action all that was necessary in the positioning of the Merkabah with the atmosphere of Earth. This was totally accomplished about five days past. Now there will be experienced by the planet a totally different vibration of Unity, and destruction of false objectives. The news today of the East Germany free passage decision is typical of that which shall follow throughout world circles and international problems. Members of Merkabah will be dispatched to every existing problem that challenges peace on Earth. There will be an increase in successful overtures against the drug traffic that prevails. Power will be on the side of right and the need of the Earth for balance. Many thousands of Divine Emissaries are now released to penetrate the Earth's darker situations and social problems. This will be a coming year of demonstrations and the voice of the people will be heard throughout the globe as never before. Even the unaware will begin to notice the trend toward change everywhere, to one of freedom. Unofficial vigilantes shall arise more and more in this freedom to govern themselves in honor.

Our own stations of readiness are positioned in continual alert

155

to report wherever needed at this time. I would like to remind you, Dear Tuella, that because of this action that was undertaken in Yucatan the general outreach for 200 miles around the Gulf Coast was immediately effected by the inundations and vibrations of a positive nature. This has resulted in a very major generating of cleansing influences and clearing of the areas involved.

This momentous occasion of October 13, 1989, was revealed to the Solar Team by the Father very early in the year, but the specific time remained always the same. We wanted to see the ripening of Universal Love to a certain degree before opening the Power Point. Now "it is finished," as above, so below, and one of the greatest days in the history of Earth has taken place. I Am Jesus, your Friend and Brother.

Benediction

By
Our Heavenly Father

My Child I AM with You,

I send you the depth of the Love of MY Being. I breathe into your form MY Healing Perfection. This, too, shall pass and you shall rise in great strength on the wings of the Eagle.

Let us begin by rejoicing together, with the entire Hosts of Heaven, that the work is done. The greatest vehicle of the Dove Command now rests on its mission place, attached to its Cosmic Portion, so long hidden and idle beneath the great waters. Now is the hour, and this desire of MY Heart is now accomplished and I have released that which is to follow.

The Light will flow easier, the darkness will thicken...to each his own. The hidden faith of the just and the unjust shall be unveiled by MY Love for them.

Walk now in the expectancy of MY momentary Victory. MOTHER hath made Herself ready and She shall shake off her suffering and sorrow. Put upon Thee Thy White Robe and draw nigh within Thy Heart to THE THRONE where MY Family, where MY Arms await Thee, to share Our Joy. So shall it be forever.

These are MY Thoughts this day Beloved One. To hold in Your HEART, To GUIDE YOU INTO Your pattern for the future days that are held securely in MY HANDS. ALL of you who have entered this Teamwork with ME, are the living embodiment of the Great Solar Cross, encircled and held as ONE, with MY Love for You and ALL of MY Children and MY Beautiful GARDEN...Earth. And so it is.

I AM, THY FATHER, MOTHER... CREATOR

Tuella

11